A Newcomer's Guide to Building a Life in North America

----- *Book 1* -----

SURVIVING THE FIRST 90 DAYS

The Essential Survival Guide for Newcomers in the US and Canada

ALAIN POUGOM

PROPEL PUBL

Published by **Propel Freedom Publishing**
An imprint of **Propel IT Solutions LLC**

First Edition
ISBN: 979-8-9958594-0-6
Printed in the United States of America

Disclaimer

This book is provided for informational and educational purposes only. While every effort has been made to ensure accuracy, the author and publisher make no guarantees regarding the completeness or applicability of the information to any individual situation.

Nothing in this book should be considered legal, financial, medical, or other professional advice. Readers are encouraged to seek guidance from qualified professionals based on their specific needs.

The author and publisher are not responsible for any losses, damages, or outcomes resulting from the use or application of the information presented in this book.

Every journey is different. Use this book as a guide—not as a substitute for professional advice, especially in areas such as immigration, employment, credit, and financial decisions.

Epigraph

"Every journey starts in your mind—but it only becomes real the moment you decide to move".

— A.P.

Dedication

To every newcomer who stepped into the unknown with nothing but courage,
to every parent who sacrificed comfort for their children's future,
and to every dreamer who refused to give up.

This book is for you.

Your journey builds nations.
Your resilience creates hope.
Your first 90 days are only the beginning.

Foreword

Years ago, I was working with a young man who was stressed out that he couldn't make ends meet on his modest income. He shared an apartment with roommates and didn't do anything flashy. After a while, I broke from our usual counseling territory and asked a few practical questions. It turns out he was getting take-out for breakfast, lunch, and dinner every day. He thought that was just what you did when you lived in the city. No one had ever told him otherwise. A simple adjustment saved hundreds of dollars a month and lowered his stress level significantly.

When you're building a life, for the first time or in a new city, there are lots of little decisions and strategies to consider. How do you find a job? Do you need a car? Where should you live? How do you open a bank account? How is your medical care handled? And often, like that young man I was working with, you don't know what you don't know.

Every year, hundreds of thousands of immigrants do an extreme version of this, something that takes more courage than most people will ever be asked to summon: they leave everything they know—their language, family, networks, sense of belonging—and start over in a country that doesn't yet know their name. It's a leap of faith into the literal unknown. A remarkably brave act.

Some are doctors, engineers, or business owners back home and now feel, for the first time in years, like beginners. Some arrive with nothing but their family's hope. If you are one of them, newly in the United States or Canada with a suitcase and a phone (that might not be connected to local cell service yet), trying to figure out how anything works here, *Surviving the First 90 Days* is written for you.

This book is like having a local friend to help with those early choices. A very knowledgeable local friend who's been through the same challenges and knows what you need to do, and what you don't know you don't know.

Alain Pougom arrived in the United States with a master's degree in IT, three children, limited English, no car, and no credit history. He figured out the system one step at a time. Every page reflects that hard-won wisdom. Alain shares best practices to help you avoid unnecessary mistakes, offers firm counsel to make sure you have a solid foundation before aiming for bigger opportunities with bigger risks, and holds your hand through potential challenges—telling you where to go and how to ask for help. He even provides phone scripts to guide you in advocating for yourself.

Surviving the First 90 Days is organized around a simple premise: your first three months in North America are the most critical. Get them right and you build a foundation. Drift through them without a plan and you burn through your savings, your confidence, and your options. The book gives you the operational details that make it possible to succeed, with checklists and strategies and cautions and encouragement.

It begins where every newcomer actually begins: with documents. Before you can work, rent an apartment, or open a bank account, you need the right papers. It covers identity documents—your Social Security or Social Insurance Number, state or provincial ID, driver's license—explaining not just what you need but why, and what happens when you delay.

Then comes housing, with guidance on avoiding scams, understanding your rights as a tenant, and choosing location over style when you're just starting out. Banking advice covers account options, how to avoid excessive fees, and why your credit score starts accumulating—for better or worse—from the moment you arrive. In the employment section, Alain gives you a clear strategy for finding income fast while lining up something better or transferring your credentials from back home. He also addresses an issue most job guides skip entirely: the unwritten cultural rules of the North American workplace.

The healthcare chapter is essential reading especially for those coming to the US, since the country's system has financial traps for those who are used to public coverage or very different cost structures. You'll understand things like deductibles, copays, and out-of-pocket maximums, and how to make sure care you seek is covered, before you need to know.

Though I've only lived in another country for a few years of my life, I've been through many transitions—most relevantly, moving cross-country to a new city without local support. As I read this book, I kept thinking two things: *I wish I'd had this advice*, and *that's exactly what I did and what I suggest to others.*

The strategies and stories in this book are powerful because they are grounded in how the system actually functions. Alain Pougom wrote the guide he needed when he arrived and didn't have. He's been the person sleeping on a friend's couch, taking three buses to a warehouse job, looking at a bank balance in week three and feeling genuine fear. When he tells you not to rush into a car purchase, or to read the fine print on a bank account application, or to show up five minutes early to work, these are things he learned the hard way, or watched others learn, and is now passing on.

What you hold in your hands is the result of Alain's experience: a clear, practical, honest companion for the most difficult and most important chapter of your new life.

It was an honor to have a small role in helping bring *Surviving the First 90 Days* to print, so that more new immigrants can have access to Alain's wisdom. This is a lot of practical knowledge captured in a short, clear text—and for the people who need it most, it could change everything.

Phil Fox Rose
writer, editor, spiritual director
Seattle, WA
June 2026

Acknowledgments

Writing this book has been one of the most meaningful journeys of my life. It would not have been possible without the people who stood beside me with love, patience, and strength.

- **To my wife, Blandine Pougom**—thank you for your unwavering belief in me. Your support carried me through late nights, endless revisions, and moments of doubt. You are the quiet force behind this work.
- **To my four boys**—you are my greatest inspiration. Your resilience, curiosity, and dreams remind me every day why this journey matters. This book is part of the legacy I am building for you.
- **To my mother, Suzanne Ngueukam**—thank you for your continued support and belief in me, even from afar. The distance between us is not easy, but your love has never felt far.
- **In loving memory of my father, Jean-Baptiste Yossa**—his values are woven into every page. Though he is no longer with us, the principles of integrity and hard work he modeled are the foundation of this book.
- **To Phil Fox Rose**—thank you for your editorial insight and guidance. You brought clarity, structure, and excellence to these pages.
- **To every newcomer whose story shaped this work**—your courage and determination live in every chapter.
- **To the friends who welcomed me when I first arrived in North America**—thank you for showing me the true meaning of community.
- **To my extended family**—your sacrifices and belief in me carried me through the hardest transitions. Your love is the foundation beneath everything I build.

And finally, to you—the reader: thank you for trusting me to walk with you through your first 90 days.

Your new life begins with what you do next.

Contents

INTRODUCTION

The Warrior's Transition

Dear friend,

If you are holding this book, you have just completed one of the most courageous acts a human being can perform: you have left behind everything familiar to start a new life in a foreign land.

When you first step off the plane or cross the border, your world spins. Everything from the way people speak to the way the buses run feels slightly "off." You may be a doctor, an engineer, or a business owner back home, but here you feel like a student again, trying to learn the basic rules of survival.

This "spinning" is normal. It is the feeling of your old life fading and your new life beginning. But you will not stay in the spinning world forever. You will need a foundation.

The 90-Day Window

Your first three months after arriving are the most critical. This is the "Gap", the space between who you were and who you are becoming. If you navigate these 90 days with discipline, you will build that foundation as a launchpad for your future. If you drift through them without a plan, you risk burning through your savings and your spirit.

This book is not a collection of theories. It is a tactical manual. I wrote it to provide the guide I wish I had when I first arrived in North America. It is designed to move you from chaos to stability by focusing on the "four walls" of your new life: shelter, food, communications, and transportation.

The Roadmap at a Glance

- **Phase 1 — Survival (Days 1–30)**
    - Secure legal ID
    - Open a bank account
    - Protect your "Survival Cash"
- **Phase 2 — Stabilization (Days 31–60)**
    - Find your "Survival Job"
    - Secure a safe place to live
- **Phase 3 — Building (Days 61–90)**
    - Start the "Bridge" to your professional career
    - Protect your financial future

You Are a Builder

You are currently in the Survival phase, which might mean taking a job that feels *below* you or living in a space that is smaller than you are used to.

Do not be discouraged. A tall building requires a deep foundation. This book will help you dig that foundation so that your future in North America can stand strong for decades to come.

Take a deep breath. You have already done the hardest part. You showed up. Now, let's get to work on the first 30 days.

Welcome home.

With respect and solidarity,

— Alain Pougom

CHAPTER 1

Welcome to Your New Beginning

Congratulations on taking this courageous step. Arriving in a new country is an incredible achievement, but I know the truth: it can also feel like the world is spinning too fast. You have left behind your familiar routines, your family, and your safety nets—to step into a system that operates by a completely different set of rules.

The first **90 days** is your foundation. It isn't about achieving perfection; it is about establishing **stability**.

By the end of this chapter, you will have a roadmap for the first stage of this: your first few weeks. You will be ready to secure housing, open your first bank account, move around your new city, and find that critical first job.

Finding Your Feet: Essential Documents

Before you can work, rent an apartment, or even open a bank account, you need the right documents. Without them, many doors remain closed.

Here's what you must secure first:

- **National ID — Social Security Number (SSN) in the US; Social Insurance Number (SIN) in Canada:** This is your official ID for employment, taxes, and banking. Apply immediately if you don't have it.
- **State/Provincial ID:** Not everyone can get a driver's license immediately. If not, a state/provincial ID helps prove your identity for daily activities.
- **Driver's License:** If you plan to drive, research the licensing rules for your state or province. Many require a written test and vision test, then often a few weeks holding a learner's permit to practice or take lessons, and finally a driving exam. Don't rush. Plan around your work schedule.
- **Work Authorization / Status Documents:** Keep these handy, as your employer will need them to confirm your eligibility.

Housing First Steps—Safe and Affordable

Some of us stay temporarily with a friend or family member while sorting documents. That's okay. Your first weeks are about stability, not perfection.

Finding a permanent home is a marathon, not a sprint.

- **Start small and short-term** — It is perfectly normal to stay with friends, family, or in a temporary rental, such as an Airbnb or extended-stay hotel. This buffer time allows you to research neighborhoods and transit without committing to a year-long contract.

- **Know the requirements** — Most landlords ask for government ID, proof of income, and a security deposit. Because you are new, some may ask for a larger deposit or a cosigner.
- **Watch for scams (rule #1)** — Never wire money or pay a deposit until you have physically walked through the apartment and signed a written lease. If a deal looks too good to be true, it is.

Banking First Steps—Securing Your Money

Money is freedom but keeping it in your pocket is a risk. You need a safe place for your funds immediately.

- **Checking vs. savings** — A *checking account* is for your daily life (paying rent, buying groceries). A *savings account* is where you tuck away money for emergencies.
- **Hidden costs** — Ask about monthly maintenance fees, minimum balance requirements, and ATM fees. Many banks offer newcomer packages with fees waived for the first year. Always ask for these!
- **Debit vs. credit** — A debit card spends the money you already have in your checking account. A credit card builds a history (which we will discuss later in this book series). For now, focus on mastering your debit card.

Transportation Without a Car

In North America, no car does not mean no movement.

- **Embrace public transit** — If it's available where you are living, public transit is the most cost-effective way to explore your new city. Download apps like Google Maps and Moovit. They provide real-time bus and train schedules.

- **Rideshare services** — Uber, Lyft, and local alternatives fill the gaps in public transit coverage, but they can be expensive for daily commutes.
- **Tempted to get a car?** — Don't rush into a car loan. Use public transit when available for the first few months to save money.
- **The two-wheel advantage** — If your job is within walking distance (1 to 2 miles, or 1.6 to 3.2 kilometers) from your home, a bicycle is often faster and cheaper than the bus.
    - The refurbished route — Check local bike co-ops or nonprofits that sell tuned-up used bikes for $50–$100.
    - Safety first — In North America, many cities require helmets by law. Always use a front white light and a back red light if riding after dark to stay visible to cars.
    - Secure your asset — Invest in a sturdy U-lock. A cheap cable lock is easily cut, and losing your bike is a major budget setback in building up your stability.

Car and Car Insurance Basics

In North America, a car is often a necessity for work, but for a newcomer it can also be a significant financial trap. During your first 90 days, you should transition from public transit to vehicle ownership *only* when your Four Walls are stable.

Buying Your First Used Car Safely

Don't rush. A bad car can wipe out your savings in repair bills.

- **The 3-Month Rule** — Wait until you have at least three months of stable income before committing to a car payment or a large purchase.
- **Car inspection is mandatory** — Never buy a used car without having a local mechanic give it a *pre-purchase inspection (PPI)*. It

usually costs $100–$150, but will prevent you from buying a car with hidden defects that will lead to expensive repair bills down the road.

- **Check the history** — Use the car's vehicle identification number (VIN) to get a vehicle history report from Carfax or AutoCheck. This will tell you if the car was ever in a flood or totaled in an accident.

The Cost of the Road (Insurance)

Owning a car costs more than just the purchase price, repairs, and fuel; insurance is a legal requirement. In most US states and Canadian provinces, you cannot even register a car in your name without proof of insurance.

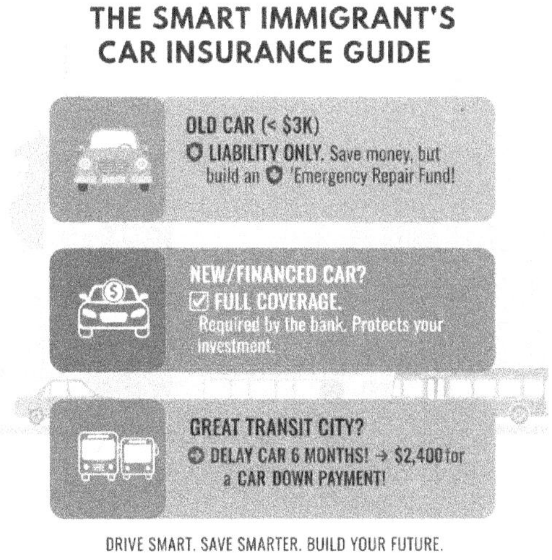

Understanding Coverage

- **Liability (minimum)** — This covers damage you cause to *others*. It is the cheapest option and the legal minimum. If you crash, the insurance pays for the other person's car, but you get $0 to fix yours.

- **Full coverage** — This covers your car as well. If you take a loan to buy the car, the bank will *require* you to have this.

The "Newcomer Rate" Reality

Prepare for sticker shock. Because you have no local driving history, you are treated as a new driver, regardless of how many years you have been driving back home.

- **Budget** — Expect to pay *up to $300 per month* for insurance alone in your first year, depending on your coverage and city.
- **The no-claims document hack** — If possible, bring an official letter from your previous insurance company at home stating how many years you drove without an accident. Some North American companies will give you a discount for this. But most of us may not be qualified for it.

Shop Around

Insurance prices are not fixed. Call at least three different companies or find an insurance broker who can show you a comparison of ten different companies at once.

Tool: The Newcomer Insurance Phone Script

Use this script when calling insurance companies or brokers. Being prepared can save you hundreds of dollars.

The Introduction:

> "Hi, my name is [your name]. I am a newcomer to the country and I'm looking for an auto insurance quote. I want to make sure I am getting any **newcomer or first-time driver discounts** you offer."

The Critical Claims History Question:

"I have [number] years of driving experience in my home country of [country]. I have a **claims experience letter** showing a clean driving record. Do you accept international history to help lower my premium?"

The Bundle Strategy:

"I also need renter's insurance for my apartment. If I buy both policies from you, what is the **multi-policy discount**?"

The Coverage Selection:

- *If the car is old:* "I only need **liability coverage** at the [state/provincial] minimum to keep my costs low." (It is recommended to also have **Uninsured motorist (UM) coverage** in this case to protect you financially if you are hit by a driver who lacks insurance or is underinsured).
- *If the car is newer:* "I need a quote for **full coverage** (collision and comprehensive) with a $1,000 deductible." *(Note: A higher deductible lowers your monthly payment!)*

The Closing Question:

"Are there any other discounts available? For example, for taking a local defensive driving course, using winter tires, or using a telematics app that tracks safe driving?"

💡 Pro Tip—Don't Just Call One

Insurance rates for newcomers vary wildly. Company A might charge you $100/month, while Company B (which specializes in newcomers) might charge $70/month for the exact same coverage. **Always get at least three quotes.**

Tool: The "Can I Afford It?" Monthly Car Worksheet

Before you sign any papers, fill out this estimated monthly budget. If the total cost is more than 20% of your take-home pay, you aren't ready for a car yet.

Expense Category	Estimated Monthly Cost	Notes
Loan Payment	$______	Enter $0 if you are paying cash.
Insurance	$______	Get quotes *before* you buy the car.
Fuel (Gas)	$______	Estimate based on commuting distance per month, mileage rating, and fuel price.
Maintenance	$______	Save at least $25/month for tires, oil, etc. (varies by location)
Parking/Tolls	$______	Does your apartment charge for a spot? Are there tolls on your commuting route?
TOTAL MONTHLY	$______	

Your First Job: Survival Before Preference

Your first job in your new country may not be your dream career. That is okay.

- **The "Survival Job":** Entry-level work in retail, delivery, and at warehouses provides immediate cash flow and local experience. It's a stepping stone, not a destination.

- **The Resume Shift:** Employers in the US and Canada expect a very specific resume style. Focus on your skills, achievements, and reliability rather than relying on foreign job titles.
- **Beware of Scams:** No legitimate employer will ever ask you to pay them for a job or to "reimburse" them for equipment.
- **Workplace etiquette:** Observe, learn, and adapt. Every workplace has its own culture.

🛠 The Newcomer's Survival Toolkit

Tool: The Four Walls Budget Template

In your first 30 days, ignore luxury. Focus on these four categories to ensure you stay afloat.

Category	Goal	Notes
Food	Groceries Only	Avoid restaurants for the first 60 days.
Shelter	Rent & Utilities	Your #1 priority is to keep a roof over your head.
Transportation (Transit)	Bus/Train Pass/ Bike/Car	The cost of getting to interviews and work.
Communication	Phone/Internet	Essential for job hunting and staying in touch.

Tool: The Digital Navigator

Download these three essentials tonight:

1. **Transit app:** Google Maps, Citymapper, Moovit, or a transit app for your location.
2. **Banking app:** To monitor your balance daily.

3. **Translation app** *(if English is not your first language)*: for reading signs and documents. Google Translate is a good option.

Tool: The Used Car Inspection Checklist

Take this with you when you go to look at a vehicle. If a seller refuses to let you check these items, walk away.

1. The "Under the Hood" Basics

- ☐ **Fluids:** Pull the oil dipstick. If the oil is milky or has white foam, the engine is likely damaged.
- ☐ **The ground:** Look under the car after it has been running for five minutes. Are there fresh puddles of oil or green/orange coolant?
- ☐ **Battery:** Check for heavy white or blue corrosion on the terminals.

2. The Exterior and Safety

- ☐ **Tires:** Check the tread depth. If the tires are bald (very little tread), you'll immediately need to spend $400–$800 for a new set.
- ☐ **Panel gaps:** Do the gaps between the doors and the body look even? If one side is wider than the other, the car was likely in a major accident.
- ☐ **Lights:** Test the blinkers, high beams, and brake lights.

3. The Test Drive

- ☐ **Brakes:** Do you feel pulsing or hear a squealing sound when you stop?
- ☐ **Alignment check:** On a flat, empty road, let go of the steering wheel for one second. If the car pulls immediately to the left or right, that's an alignment problem.

☐ **Electronics:** Test the air conditioning, heater (critical for winter!), and all window control buttons.

Practical Tools for Your Transition

90-Day "First Essentials" Checklist

Use this timeline to prioritize your tasks so you don't feel pressured to do everything at once.

Timeline	Priority Task	Completed
Week 1	Apply for SSN/SIN and open a basic checking account.	☐
Week 2	Secure what you need for local phone use (SIM card/phone plan/new phone) and map out public transit routes.	☐
Week 3	Apply for a State/Provincial ID and update your resume to local standards.	☐
Month 1	Secure stable housing and establish a Survival Budget for basics.	☐
Month 2	Secure first employment and begin building a small emergency fund.	☐
Month 3	Apply for a secured credit card to start building a local credit history and credit score.	☐

The Digital Safe Box Strategy

In your new country, losing your physical documents can be a disaster.

- **Strategy:** Use a secure cloud storage tool (like Google Drive, iCloud, or Dropbox) to create a "digital safe box."

- **Action:** Scan your passport, visa, birth certificate, and vaccination records.
- **Why:** If your wallet or bag is lost, you will have the reference numbers and copies ready to present to authorities to get replacements.

Expense Tracker (The Envelope Method)

Before you have a banking app, use a simple notebook or a note on your phone to categorize every dollar spent in the first 30 days. Divide your spending into three "buckets":

1. **Fixed:** rent and phone bill
2. **Flexible:** groceries and transit
3. **Setup:** one-time costs like apartment deposits and winter clothing

Pro Tip

Download a translation app with a camera feature so you can point your phone at utility bills, lease agreements, and grocery labels to translate them into your native language in real time.

Your First-Month Survival Budget

The goal of this budget is not to grow your wealth; it is to ensure your Four Walls (shelter, food, communications, and transportation) are covered while you are finding your footing.

One-Time Startup Costs

These are the expenses you pay once, when you arrive. They are often the biggest expenses of the first 90 days.

Item	Estimated Cost	Actual Cost
Housing Deposit (Security, First, and Last)	$	$
Utility Deposits (Electric, Water, and Gas)	$	$
Document Fees (IDs, Licenses, and Permits)	$	$
Essential Household Goods (Bedding, Cookware)	$	$
Total Startup Costs	$	$

Monthly Essential Expenses

These are the bills you must pay for a month to stay stable.

Category	Monthly Budget	Actual Cost
Rent or Other Housing	$	$
Groceries (Avoid eating out in first month)	$	$
Public Transit Pass and/or Fuel	$	$
Phone Plan (Data is essential for GPS and finding jobs)	$	$
Laundry and Personal Hygiene	$	$
Emergency Fund (Even $20 helps)	$	$
Total Monthly Expenses	$	$

The Survival Calculation

Use this simple formula to see where you stand:

Core Monthly Expenses = Housing + Food + Utilities + Healthcare + Transportation + Phone/Internet

Total Monthly Income – Core Monthly Expenses = Your Monthly Buffer Cash

Newcomer Strategy — The Rice and Beans Rule: For your first 30 days, try to keep your flexible spending (entertainment, luxury food, new clothes) as close to *zero* as possible. Once you have your first three weekly paychecks in the bank, you can begin to breathe easier and adjust these categories.

How to use this tool:

- **Be honest** — Write down every coffee and bus fare. Small leaks sink big ships.
- **Save receipts** — In many countries, certain relocation expenses may be tax-deductible later.
- **Use cash for groceries** — If you are worried about overspending on a debit card, take out your exact grocery budget in cash. When the cash is gone, the shopping ends.

Real-Life Illustrations: Two Paths to Stability

To understand how these first 90 days look in practice, let's look at two different approaches to the same journey.

The Story of Mateo — Mateo arrived with high hopes but felt the pressure to "look successful" immediately. He spent his initial savings on a used car that turned out to be unreliable and skipped the research on local banking. By day 45, his car had broken down, he had no savings for the repair, and, because he hadn't secured his official ID yet, he couldn't apply for a stable job he had found. He felt stuck.

The Story of Sarah (and Me) — I arrived with just two suitcases and no car. Like my friend Sarah, I focused on the "invisible" wins first. Sarah stayed in a small, shared room and used the bus every day for two months. She spent her evenings at the local library—using their free Wi-Fi to study for her local certifications and researching how to build a credit score.

While others saw her taking the bus as a sign she was struggling, for Sarah it was a strategy. By day 60, she had a clean financial record, $1,500 saved from a survival job, and her official state ID. When a great job opening appeared in month three, she was ready. She wasn't just surviving; she was *prepared*.

Chapter Reflection

Take a moment to sit with these questions. Be honest with yourself—this is your foundation.

- **What is my biggest unknown right now?** Is it how the buses work, or how to open a bank account? Identifying this reduces vague anxiety.
- **Am I rushing to look settled?** Are you tempted to buy things you don't need yet just to feel "normal"?
- **Who is my support system?** List one local person or organization you can call for advice on local rules.

Action Steps

In your first seven days, do not try to do everything. Focus this week only on these five "launchpad" tasks.

- ☐ **The Document Audit:** Scan your passport, visa, and birth certificate and email them to yourself today. Place them in one waterproof folder.
- ☐ **The Local "Map Out":** Identify the nearest grocery store, bank, and library. Use Google Maps to find the walking or bus routes to each.
- ☐ **The Identity Phase:** Book appointments for your SSN/SIN and state/province IDs. These offices often have long wait times.
- ☐ **The Banking Baseline:** Visit a local bank. Ask specifically about no-monthly-fee accounts for newcomers.
- ☐ **The Survival Budget:** Use the template provided above to list exactly how much buffer cash you have and what your must-pay bills are for the next 30 days.

CHAPTER 2

The Keys to the Kingdom — Securing Your Identity

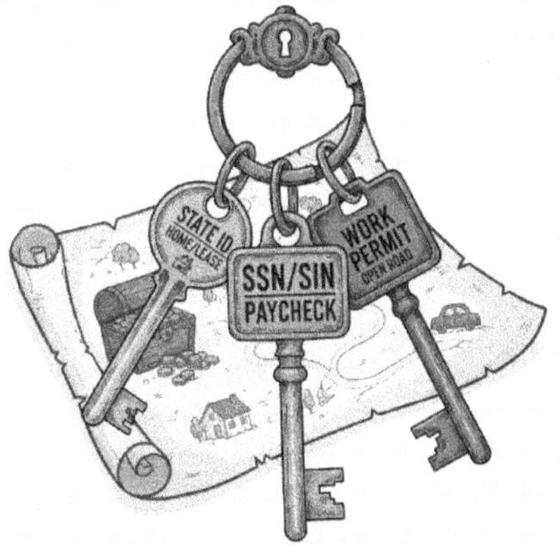

DOCUMENTS: THE KEYS TO YOUR FUTURE

In your home country, you knew exactly who you were. Here, the system doesn't know you yet. To the government, banks, and employers, you are only as real as the papers in your hand. Think of your documents as a *set of keys*. One opens the door to a paycheck, another to a home, and a third to the open road. Without these keys, you are locked out of the very life you came here to build. This chapter isn't just about paperwork; it's about claiming your legal access to life in your new country.

The Master Key: SSN (US) or SIN (Canada)

This number is essential. It is your financial fingerprint. You need it to get paid, to pay taxes, and to access government benefits.

- **The Process** — Visit a Social Security Administration (SSA) or Service Canada office. Bring your passport, immigration visa, and work permit. It usually takes *2–4 weeks* to arrive in the mail.
- **Safety Warning** — *Never* carry this card in your wallet. Once you receive it, memorize the number and hide the card in a safe place. Identity theft is real, and this number is the primary target.

The Daily Key: State or Provincial ID

You cannot carry your passport everywhere; the risk of losing it is too great. A local ID is your daily identification. It proves you live where you say you live.

- **Why it matters** — You'll need it to pick up a package at the post office, enter certain buildings, and even buy a local SIM card.

💡 Pro Tip

If you aren't ready for a driving test, apply for a **"Non-Driver Photo ID."** It looks like a license but requires no test.

The Freedom Key: Driver's License

In North America in many cities, a car isn't a luxury; it's a survival tool.

- **Strategy** — Most regions have a written Knowledge Test first, after which you receive a temporary permit to use while preparing to take the road test before receiving your full license.

- **Secret** — Many states allow you to take the written test in your native language. Ask about this before you sit down!

The Stability Key: Work Authorization

Your work permit, Employment Authorization Document (EAD), Green Card, Permanent Residence (PR) card, or worker visa document is your right to earn.

Keep it Current — Set a phone calendar alert for *6 months **before*** your document expires. Renewals can take a long time; never let your status lapse while you are working.

The Danger Key: What Happens If Your Documents Expire

Let me be direct with you about something that too many newcomers learn the hard way. Securing your documents is step one. Protecting them—and keeping them current—is the step most people forget. In today's environment, an expired work permit, visa, or residency document is not just an inconvenience. It can interrupt your employment, delay your plans, and create unnecessary stress during a period when stability matters most. This is not meant to scare you. It is meant to prepare you. Think of your immigration documents like car insurance. You hope you do not need to think about them often, but when the moment comes, they must be valid and accessible.

The Three Expiry Traps Newcomers Fall Into:

- **The "I'll Handle It Later" Trap** — Renewals take time. Processing delays happen. If you wait until the month your document expires, you may already be behind schedule.

- **The "I Didn't Know It Expired" Trap** — Life gets busy. Working, studying, raising children, adapting to a new environment. Expiry dates are easy to overlook.
- **The "Someone Else Is Tracking It" Trap** — Do not assume your employer, school, or anyone else is monitoring your immigration deadlines. Your status is your responsibility.

The 6-Month Rule

Set a calendar reminder six months before any important document expires.

This gives you time to:

- Gather required paperwork
- Save for filing fees
- Review eligibility requirements
- Submit renewal applications early

The 90-Day Rule

Set a second reminder three months before expiration.

At this stage:

- Confirm your renewal has been submitted
- Check receipt notices or confirmation numbers
- Follow up if necessary

Many problems happen not because people were careless, but because they started too late.

💡 Pro Tip

Build Your Expiry Alert System

For every document in your Power Folder, create two reminders:

- **Alert 1** — 6 months before expiry "Start renewal process for [document]"
- **Alert 2** — 3 months before expiry "Confirm renewal submitted for [document]"

This takes less than five minutes and can save you months of disruption.

The Replacement Key: What to Do If Documents Are Lost or Stolen

Documents can disappear faster than you expect. A stolen backpack, a misplaced wallet, a move, a fire, a flooded basement. This is why organization matters. If an important document goes missing, follow these steps immediately.

If Your Passport Is Lost or Stolen:

- Report it to local authorities if theft is involved
- Contact your country's embassy or consulate
- Begin replacement procedures immediately

If Your SSN/SIN or Insurance Document Card Is Missing:

- Stay calm
- Verify whether you actually need a physical copy and start the replacement process
- Write down and store your number in a safe location

If Your Work Permit or Authorization Document Is Missing:

- Report the issue promptly
- Begin replacement procedures through the appropriate immigration agency

- Notify your employer if relevant

The Golden Rule of Document Loss

The moment you realize a document is missing:

- **Step 1** — Access your Digital Safe Box to retrieve scanned copies and document numbers.
- **Step 2** — Begin the replacement or reporting process immediately.

This is why your Digital Safe Box is not optional. It is your backup system.

🛠 The Newcomer's Identity Toolkit

Tool: The Power Folder System

Don't just throw your papers in a drawer. Create a physical "**power folder.**" (An accordion-style file works best.) Label the tabs:

- **Identity** – Passports, Birth Certificates
- **Immigration** – Visas, SSN/SIN cards, EADs
- **Residency** – Lease agreements, utility bills (to prove where you live)
- **Health** – Vaccination records, insurance

Tool: Digital Safe Box

Download a scanning app to your phone (like Adobe Scan or Microsoft Lens).

- Scan every document in your power folder.

- Save them to a password-protected folder in the cloud (Google Drive/iCloud). If a fire or theft happens, you will have the numbers and copies ready to go.

Tool: Document Expiry Master Tracker

Use this table to track every major document you own.

Document	Issue Date	Expiry Date	6-Month Alert Set?	Physical Copy Stored?	Digital Copy Saved?
Passport			☐	☐	☐
Visa / Entry Stamp			☐	☐	☐
Work Permit / EAD			☐	☐	☐
Green Card / PR Card			☐	☐	☐
State / Provincial ID			☐	☐	☐
Driver's License			☐	☐	☐
Health Insurance Card			☐	☐	☐

Real-Life Illustration: The Cost of Waiting

I remember meeting two friends, Elias and Marc, who arrived in the same period, only two weeks apart. On his first Monday, Elias from Ghana decided to get his SSN. He was bored and frustrated waiting in line at the Social Security office, but he got his receipt and started the process. Marc from Gabon decided to "rest" for a while and explore the city first, thinking he'd handle paperwork later. When a local warehouse offered them both a job starting immediately, Elias showed his SSN receipt and started work the following Friday. Marc had to wait for an appointment at the Social Security office. By the time Marc got things sorted, the job opening was gone.

The Lesson: In North America, *paperwork is key.* Do the boring stuff first so you can do the exciting stuff later.

Real-Life Illustration: The Expired Card

I want to tell you about Thomas. He arrived from Benin and quickly found work at a logistics company. By month six, he finally felt stable. Rent was paid. Bills were manageable. Life was starting to make sense. But Thomas made one quiet mistake. He never set a renewal reminder, assuming that his employer's HR team would notify him if something needed attention. That did not happen. Months later, during a routine employment verification review, his work authorization had already expired. His employer had no choice but to suspend his employment until he could provide updated documentation. What should have been a simple renewal turned into months of lost income, stress, and instability.

Later, Thomas said: "I built everything on a foundation I forgot to maintain."

The lesson: Documents are not a one-time task. They are a system you must manage continuously while building your new life.

Chapter Reflection

Take a deep breath. Bureaucracy can feel like a mountain, but you climb it one step at a time.

- **Priority Check:** Which document is holding me back from my next goal (e.g., "I can't get a job without my SSN/SIN")?

- **Storage Check:** If I had to leave my house in five minutes due to an emergency, do I know exactly where my passport and SSN/SIN are?
- **Patience Check:** Am I frustrated by the wait times? Remember, the system is slow, but your persistence will yield results.

Action Steps

Complete these in order. Do not skip a step.

- ☐ **Step 1:** Locate the nearest Social Security Administration (SSA) or Service Canada office on Google Maps today.
- ☐ **Step 2:** Download the driver's guide PDF for your state/province. Read five pages before bed tonight.
- ☐ **Step 3:** Gather two *proofs of residency*. These usually include utility bills and bank statements with your name and current address. Most ID processes require two of these.
- ☐ **Step 4:** Create your **Digital Safe Box**. Scan your passport and visa and any other work documents a**nd upload** them to a secure cloud folder.
- ☐ **Step 5:** Fill in your Document Expiry Master Tracker.
- ☐ **Step 6:** Set your 6-month and 3-month renewal alerts for all important documents.

Each document you secure is a building block for stability. Completing these steps is not just paperwork, it's freedom. Take action, and you'll see doors opening in your first 90 days.

CHAPTER 3

Housing 101 — Finding Your Safe Harbor

Your home is more than just shelter; it is your base of operations. It is where you rest, recover, and plan your next move. For a newcomer, though, the housing market can feel like a maze. Many immigrants (like me) begin on a friend's couch, or in a crowded shared room or modest basement.

There is *no shame* in a humble start. What matters during your first 90 days is *stability*, and this chapter will help you navigate the transition from "somewhere to sleep" to a place you can truly call home.

The Starting Line: Temporary Housing

Most successful newcomers don't sign a lease on day one. They use a "stepping stone" approach.

- **Staying with family or friends** — This is the most common path. It allows you to save for a deposit and learn the city.

Pro Tip

Keep the relationship healthy by setting a move-out goal date and contributing to groceries or utilities (when you can).

- **Short-term rental** — If you are on your own, look for Airbnbs with monthly discounts and extended-stay hotels. These are more expensive than apartments but don't require long-term contracts or credit checks.

Cracking the Code: Rental Requirements

In North America, landlords are gatekeepers. To open the door, you usually need:

- **Proof of Identity** — Your passport or State/Provincial ID.
- **Proof of Income** — A letter from your employer or recent pay stubs.
- **The "Newcomer Bridge"** — Because you lack a local credit history, landlords may be nervous. You can bridge this gap by offering a *higher security deposit* (if legal in your area) or a *cosigner* (someone with established credit who signs the lease with you).

The Real Cost of Living

When calculating your budget, remember that rent is just the beginning.

- **The "Big Three" Deposits:** Expect to pay the first month's rent, the last month's rent, and a security deposit (for possible damages).
- **Utilities:** Ask the landlord, "Are utilities included?" If not, you must budget in whatever isn't included, such as electricity, heating, water, and internet.
- **Renter's Insurance:** This is often required and very affordable (usually $15–$30 a month). It protects your belongings from fire or theft.

Safety First: Avoiding the Newcomer Trap

Scammers often target immigrants because they know they are in urgent situations.

- **The Golden Rule:** Never send money (via Zelle, wire transfer, or gift card) before you have physically walked inside the apartment and met the landlord.
- **Red Flags:** Prices that are too good to be true, landlords who claim to be out of the country, and pressure to "pay now or lose it" are red flags. Walk away.

Your Safe Harbor — Tenant Rights and Safety

In North America, once you sign a lease and pay rent, you have specific legal protections. You are not just a guest in your home: you are a tenant, and the law is on your side regarding safety and privacy.

The "Basics of Life" Requirement

Your landlord is legally required to provide a home that is "habitable." This means:

- **Heat in winter** — If the temperature drops below a certain level (usually 20°C or 68°F), the landlord *must* ensure the heating system works.
- **Water and electricity** — You must have access to clean water and a safe electrical system.
- **No Pests** — It is generally the landlord's responsibility to handle infestations (like bedbugs or cockroaches) unless they can prove you caused them.

Your Right to Privacy

A landlord cannot simply walk into your apartment because they own the building.

- **Notice Period:** In most regions, the landlord must give you *24 hours' notice* before entering for repairs or inspections (always check your lease or housing contract).
- **The Exception:** They can enter without notice in a true emergency (like a fire or a burst water pipe).

Security Deposits & Scams

- **The Paper Trail:** Never pay your rent or deposit in cash without a signed receipt. If a landlord insists on "cash only," it is a major red flag.
- **Normal Wear and Tear:** You are not responsible for small scuffs on the wall or wear to an old carpet. A landlord cannot keep your deposit for "normal" use, only for actual damage you caused.

💡 Pro Tip

Use "2-1-1" — If your landlord refuses to fix a broken heater or a leaking roof, do not stop paying rent immediately (this can get you evicted). Instead, call 211, the universal number for social services in the United States and Canada. They can direct you to local tenant boards or legal aid that helps immigrants for free.

🛠 The Housing Toolkit

Tool: The Neighborhood "Vibe Check"

Before you sign a lease, use this 24-hour test.

- **Morning** — Check the commute. How long does it take to get to work via bus/train?
- **Afternoon** — Are a grocery store and laundromat within walking distance?
- **Evening** — Is the street well-lit and quiet? Do you feel safe walking to your door?

Tool: The Housing Comparison Table

Use this to compare two potential places side-by-side:

Feature	Option (House) A	Option (House) B
Monthly Rent	$	$
Utilities Included? (If not, additional expense)	Yes / No	Yes / No
Distance to Transit		
Security Deposit	$	$
Overall Safety (1-10)		

Tool: The Move-In Inspection Checklist

Perform this check the hour you get your keys. Take photos of everything on your phone as proof of the condition when you arrived.

- ☐ **Test the faucets:** Make sure the hot water works and check for leaks under the sink.
- ☐ **Flush the toilet:** Ensure it drains and refills properly.
- ☐ **Check the windows:** Do they lock securely? (This is critical for safety and heating/cooling costs.)
- ☐ **Test the appliances:** Turn on every stove burner and the oven.
- ☐ **Smoke detectors:** Press the "test" button. Your life depends on this device.
- ☐ **Look for mold:** Check the corners of the bathroom and backs of closets for black spots.

Real-Life Illustration: Stability over Style

Working in the warehouse, I had a colleague named Samuel from Liberia. He arrived with enough savings to rent a beautiful apartment downtown. He moved in immediately but didn't realize the commute to his job would take two hours and three different buses. Within three months, he was exhausted and broke from the high rent.

I met Elena from Zambia at church. Unlike Samuel, she rented a small, plain room in a basement near a major bus hub. It wasn't pretty, but her rent was low and her commute was only thirty minutes. Because she chose *stability and location* over style, she saved enough in six months to buy a used car and move into a much better neighborhood on her own terms.

Location is a multiplier. Samuel paid for a view but lost his time. Elena paid for a "launchpad" and gained her freedom.

> **Strategic Takeaway:** At this stage, your housing should be a tool that serves your job, not a luxury that drains your energy or resources. If your commute is over an hour, you aren't living; you're just traveling to and from work.

Chapter Reflection

Finding a home is emotional. Take a second to check in with yourself.

1. **Am I rushing?** Is my urge to find a "perfect" place causing me to overlook my budget?
2. **Is this sustainable?** If I lost my job tomorrow, could I afford this rent for one month?
3. **Does this location help me grow?** Does this home put me closer to jobs, community, or better transit?

Action Steps

- ☐ **Define your budget:** Calculate 30% of your expected monthly income. This is your target rent.
- ☐ **Scout three areas:** Identify three neighborhoods that are within a 45-minute transit commute to your workplace.
- ☐ **Gather your "rental packet":** Have digital copies of your ID, employment letter, and bank statement ready to email to landlords instantly.
- ☐ **Line up renter's insurance:** Call a local agency or check online to identify the provider you will use when you have a lease. It's a small price for massive peace of mind, and may be required anyway.
- ☐ **Inspect the "small things":** When viewing a place, check the water pressure, look for pests, and see if the windows lock properly.

CHAPTER 4

Banking 101 — Opening Your First Account

Your financial life in this new country truly begins the moment you open your first bank account here. In the US and Canada, a bank account is more than just a place to store money; it is your *financial identity.*

Without an account, you are "unbanked," which makes life expensive and risky. With one, you have the foundation to receive a paycheck, pay your rent, and gradually build the credit history needed for a car or a home. Let's make sure you start with a solid foundation.

Why the Cash-Only Life Is Dangerous

Many newcomers are tempted to keep their savings in cash because it feels safer or more familiar. This is a mistake for three reasons:

- **Physical Risk** — Cash can be lost, stolen, or destroyed in a fire. Once it's gone, it's gone forever.
- **No Paper Trail** — To rent an apartment or get a car, you need to prove you have money. A bank statement is your proof of stability.
- **The Cost of Convenience** — Without a bank account, you will pay high fees at check-cashing stores just to get your own money out of your paychecks.

Opening Your Account — The Checklist

Banks in the US and Canada are required by law to verify who you are. Don't be intimidated; they want your business!

What to Bring

- **Primary ID: passport**
- **State/Provincial ID or driver's license** (if available)
- **Tax ID:** SSN (US) or SIN (Canada), or if you haven't received the card yet, the official receipt showing you applied
- **Proof of address:** a lease, utility bill, or even a letter from a friend or relative confirming you are staying with them
- **A small deposit:** most banks require $25–$100 to activate the account

Checking and Savings—Your Two Best Friends

- **Checking account (the workhorse):** This is for your daily life. Your paycheck goes here, and you use your *debit card* to buy groceries and pay bills.

- **Savings account (the shield):** This is for your future. Even if you only add $10 a week here, it builds your *emergency fund.* It also earns a tiny bit of interest.

The Fee Trap—How to Keep Your Money

Banks are businesses, and they love fees. As a newcomer, you must be a fee detective. Always ask:

- **"Is there a monthly service fee?"** Look for an account that will waive this if your job direct deposits your paychecks into it.
- **"What is the minimum balance?"** If the bank requires you to keep $500 in the account to avoid a monthly fee and you drop to $499, they will charge you.
- **"Are ATM withdrawals free?"** Only use ATMs owned by your bank or included in its network to avoid $3–$5 charges.

The Invisible Score (A Warning on Credit)

In your first 90 days, you might not think about *credit.* You are focused on cash and survival. However, in North America, your *credit score* is like an add-on to your ID card. It determines if you can rent a better apartment, buy a car, and even get certain jobs.

A newcomer trap: many newcomers don't realize that phone and electric bills are reported to credit bureaus.

- **If you forget to pay** your phone bill or don't pay while disputing a charge, your credit score may drop before you even have a chance to build it up.
- **A "bad" score** can follow you for seven years. It could mean the difference on a car loan between an interest rate of 4% and 20%.

Three Simple Rules to Protect Your Credit Future

1. **Pay every bill on time.** Even if it's only $10. Set up *autopay* for every bill possible immediately.

2. **Don't apply for everything.** Every time you apply for a store credit card (like at a clothing or electronics store), your score takes a tiny hit. Wait until you understand what credit you need and where to get it.
3. **"Secured" credit cards:** Once you have a steady job, ask your bank about a *secured credit card*. For example, you give them $500 as a deposit, and they give you a card with a $500 limit. This is the safest way to start building your credit score without going into debt.

🛠 The Banking Toolkit

Tool: Newcomer Account Comparison

Most major banks (like Chase and Bank of America in the US and RBC and TD in Canada) have *newcomer programs*. Use this table to compare them before you sign:

Feature	Bank A	Bank B
Monthly Fee (e.g., $0 for 12 months; $0 with Direct Deposit		
No-fee ATM Access (e.g., many nearby, limited, none)		
Mobile App Rating (high/medium/low/none)		
Free Checks? (e.g., yes unlimited; yes, first 10; no)		

Tool: Direct Deposit Setup

The fastest way to get paid is *direct deposit.* Your money will appear in your account automatically on payday—no more waiting in line at the bank!

- **Action:** Ask your bank for a *voided check* or a *direct deposit form.*
- **Action:** Give this to your employer's HR department.

Real-Life Illustration: The $56 Lesson

When I arrived, I opened an account with a local bank and felt proud. But I didn't read the fine print. To get cash, I regularly used a convenient ATM at a gas station. Each time, the gas station charged me $3 and my bank charged me $1.64. This added up to $13.92 a week, nearly $56 a month, just to touch my own money! I was not aware this was happening until I checked my bank statement.

My friend Omar from Cameroon, whom I got to know at a community gathering, was deeply afraid of banks. He kept $2,000 under his mattress in a shared apartment. One afternoon, a small kitchen fire broke out. The fire itself didn't reach his room, but the firefighters' hoses soaked everything in the apartment. By the time he checked his hiding place, the cash was water damaged and stuck together. Some bills were ruined beyond recovery. Because it wasn't in a bank, there was no way to replace it—no protection, no insurance, no "undo" button.

A bank account isn't just a tool; it's an insurance policy for your hard work.

Chapter Reflection

Take a moment to think about your relationship with money.

1. **Do I trust the system?** If I am hesitant to use a bank, is it because of a bad experience in my home country? (Remember, in the US and Canada, deposits are government insured.)
2. **Am I "leaking" cash?** Am I paying for things in cash and losing track of where the money goes?
3. **What is my safety number?** What is the minimum amount of money I need in my savings account so I can sleep peacefully?

Action Steps

- ☐ **Research three banks.** Look for newcomer accounts in your neighborhood.
- ☐ **Gather your documents.** Put your passport, SSN/SIN (or receipt), and proof of address in an envelope.
- ☐ **Go in person.** Visit the bank when it's open and ask to speak with a personal banker.
- ☐ **Set up mobile banking.** Once you open an account, download the bank's app immediately. Check it every morning to see your balance.
- ☐ **The $20 challenge:** Transfer $20 into your savings account the moment it's open. Congratulations, you have officially started saving in your new home.

CHAPTER 5

Surviving the First 30 Days — Stability Before Growth

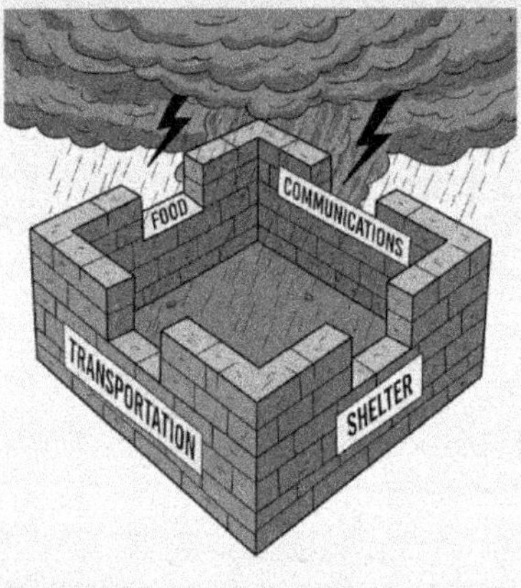

SURVIVAL MODE: PROTECTING THE ESSENTIALS.

This first month will test your discipline more than any other season of your journey. The truth is simple: *your money in the first 30 days is for survival, not enjoyment.* If you manage these early weeks with precision, you will build a foundation that saves you years of struggle. If you spend like you have already "made it," you will find yourself trapped in a cycle of debt before you even begin. Let's guide you through the essentials of the immigrant's survival mode.

The Five Non-Negotiables

Even if you arrived with some funds, you must control your *big five expenses*—the Four Walls plus setup costs. Everything else is a distraction.

- **Housing (The Base):** Focus on safety and transit access over comfort. Whether it's a shared basement or an Airbnb, it just needs to be a place to recharge.
- **Food (The Fuel):** Avoid dining out and takeout. Every restaurant meal costs as much as three days of home-cooked meals. Stick to staples: rice, beans, eggs, and seasonal vegetables.
- **Transportation (The Link):** Choose the path that drains the least. Use public transit or carpool. Only use ride-shares (e.g., Uber and Lyft) if it is a genuine emergency or for a high-stakes job interview.
- **Communication (The Tool):** You cannot find a job without a phone and internet. Get a budget-friendly prepaid plan. You don't need the newest phone yet; you need a battery that stays charged for maps and calls.
- **Essentials (The Setup):** This includes toiletries, work-specific clothing, and critical winter gear if you are in a cold climate.

The Immigrant Budget Formula

Use this simple calculation to stay focused:

Income – Survival Essentials = Amount Left for Opportunity

Opportunity includes:

- Certification and license fees
- Transportation to interviews
- Professional work uniforms or boots

If you spend your opportunity funds on comfort (like a nice dinner or a new pair of sneakers), you are literally spending your future. Small savings create big peace of mind. You'll breathe better knowing you can survive an unexpected expense.

Smart Survival Strategies

The following strategies save successful immigrants hundreds of dollars every month.

- **Thrift stores:** In the US and Canada, stores like Goodwill, Salvation Army, and Value Village are gold mines. You can find high-quality winter coats and work gear for $10–$20.
- **Batch cooking:** Cook a large batch of food (like a big pot of soup or stew) on your day off that will yield multiple meals. It saves time and prevents you from buying expensive takeout when you are tired.
- **Monthly transit passes:** Cities vary—some charge per ride, others offer day or monthly passes. A monthly pass only saves money if you ride often, like for regular interviews or commuting. Otherwise, paying per trip may cost less.
- **The winter warrior's commute:** In many parts of North America, the weather is as much a factor as the bus schedule.
  - **The "10-minute" buffer** — In winter, buses and trains are often delayed by snow. Always leave ten minutes earlier than the app suggests to ensure you aren't late for work.
  - **The gear** — Don't wait for the first blizzard. Use a thrift store to find waterproof boots and a heavy coat early. Staying dry while waiting at a bus stop is a health strategy, not just a comfort choice.
  - **Safety on ice:** Icy sidewalks are slippery. Taking short, flat-footed steps "like a penguin" can help prevent falls and the medical costs that come with them.

Your responsibility is to stabilize first so you can move to sustainability later.

Handling the Emotional Pressure

The hardest part of the first 30 days is the *pressure.*

- **The social media trap:** You will see friends posting photos of their new cars or fancy apartments. Remember, you don't know their debt. Stay in your lane.
- **Family expectations:** It is hard to say "no" when the family back home asks for money. But you must stabilize yourself first. *You cannot rescue a drowning person if you are still struggling to stay above water.*

Hear this clearly: There is no shame in starting small. The only shame is in wasting your opportunity. *Stay focused. Stay humble. Stay hungry.*

🛠 The Survival Toolkit

Tool: The "Daily Dollar" Tracker

In your first 30 days, small leaks sink big ships. Use this simple log to stay aware of every cent.

Date	Item (e.g., bus pass, coffee, groceries)	Category (e.g., transport, food, luxury)	Amount	Necessity? (Y/N)
Total			$	

Tool: The Opportunity vs. Comfort Matrix

When you are tempted to spend money, run the expense through this mental filter.

- **Opportunity (Green Light):** Professional certifications, interview clothes, transit to a job fair, a phone plan to receive employer calls. **Verdict: spend.**
- **Comfort (Red Light):** Brand-name snacks, streaming subscriptions (Netflix/Spotify), eating at a restaurant because you're tired, trendy clothing. **Verdict: wait until month 4.**

Tool: Survival Grocery List (Under $50)

If your budget is extremely tight, focus on high-calorie, low-cost items that stay fresh.

- **Proteins:** Large pack of eggs, dried beans/lentils, canned tuna, peanut butter.
- **Carbs:** Large bag of white or brown rice, oats (for breakfast), generic bread.
- **Produce:** Bag of onions, bag of potatoes, frozen mixed vegetables (lasts longer than fresh), bananas.
- **Secret Weapon:** A large bag of flour. You can make flatbread, pancakes, and thicken soups for pennies.

Real-Life Illustration: The Second-Hand Win

I remember meeting a woman named Mary who arrived in late October. She didn't have a winter coat and was about to spend $150 of her remaining $400 at a big-box store. I walked her to a local thrift store and we found a high-quality, wool coat for $12.

With the $138 she saved, she was able to pay for her internet and phone for two full months. That allowed her to stay connected to recruiters and she landed a job twenty days later. *Survival is about making your cash last long enough for your first paycheck to arrive.*

Real-Life Illustration: The $200 Tightrope

My soccer referee friend Roger told me: "I remember looking at my bank balance in my third week. After paying for my transit pass and a small room, I had less than $200 left. My chest tightened. I felt like I had made a massive mistake moving here."

That fear forced him to change. He stopped buying coffee. He walked an extra fifteen minutes to a cheaper grocery store. He tracked every single cent in a small notebook. By being extreme for just one month, he protected that $200 until his first paycheck arrived. That tiny cushion was the only thing standing between Roger and the street. *Discipline is the bridge between panic and peace.*

Chapter Reflection

1. **Is this a "want" or a "need"?** Before every purchase this month, ask yourself: *Will this help me get a job or stay healthy?* If the answer is no, put it back.
2. **Am I being honest about my spending?** Small "leaks" (snacks, small apps, subscriptions) can sink your entire budget.
3. **Do I have a "survival partner"?** Is there someone, a friend or mentor, who can keep me accountable to my budget?

Action Steps: The 30-Day Survival Plan

- ☐ **Days 1–3: The Audit.** List every dollar you have. Map out the cheapest grocery store and the bus route to the nearest library (for free internet).
- ☐ **Days 4–15: The Grind.** Apply for five jobs a day. Track every dollar spent in your phone's "notes" app.
- ☐ **Days 16–30: The Cushion.** The moment you receive your first paycheck, do not celebrate. Put $100 into your savings account immediately. This is your "freedom fund."
- ☐ **Thrift Store Run:** Go find a professional outfit for interviews for under $25.

CHAPTER 6

Finding Your First Job Quickly — Your Foothold

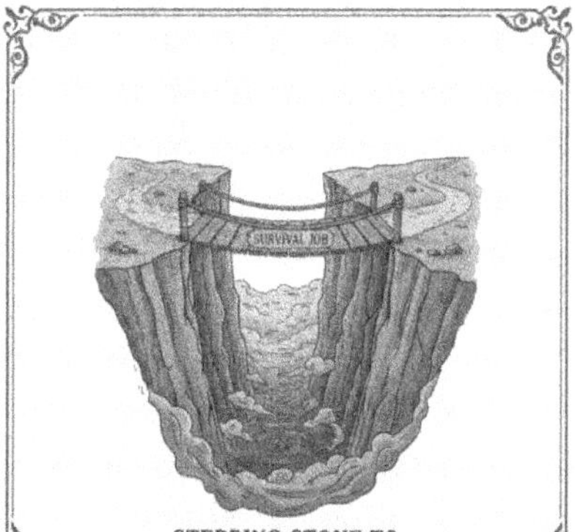

STEPPING STONE TO YOUR CAREER PATH

Now that you've stabilized your initial expenses and opened a bank account, your mission becomes simple and urgent: *Secure a stable income as quickly as possible.*

This is not about your dream career or your final destination. It is about finding your *foothold*. Once the first paycheck arrives, the heavy weight of "survival" begins to lift. Confidence, housing, and credit all become easier once you have a steady stream of income.

The Strategy: Stability Over Status

The biggest mistake newcomers make is letting pride slow them down. This is a new country, and *work is work.*

The goal is to pay rent, build local references, and learn the system. The job you take in month one is not the job you will have at the end of year one. It is simply the bridge that carries you over the initial gap.

Fast-Hiring Industries for Newcomers

Certain sectors have a high "turnover" rate, meaning they are almost always hiring and can get you working within 7 to 14 days.

Industry	Examples	Why it works
Retail & Grocery	Walmart, Target, local markets	They hire for dependability and have flexible shifts.
Logistics/Warehouse	Amazon, FedEx, UPS	Fast onboarding.
Hospitality	Hotels, fast food, cafes	Great for building local communication skills.
Maintenance	Cleaning services, janitorial	Low barrier to entry; can start almost immediately.
Caregiving	Senior care, home health	Stable pay and often offers long, consistent shifts.

The 20-Minute Resume

For your first job, managers aren't looking for high-level titles from your home country; they are looking for *reliability*.

- **Keep it to one page.**

- **Focus on transferable skills:** punctuality, teamwork, customer service, and the ability to learn fast.
- **Highlight availability.** Being able to work weekends or evenings makes you a "gold star" candidate for entry-level roles.

The Interview Fast Track

Most entry-level interviews are not designed to "trick" you. They want to know:

1. **Are you reliable?** Will you show up on time?
2. **Are you teachable?** Will you listen and learn?
3. **Are you available?** Can you work the hours they need?

Answer with confidence: "I am very reliable, I learn new systems quickly, and I am ready to start as soon as tomorrow."

Understanding Your Paycheck & Contract

When you receive a job offer, don't just look at the total number. You must understand the *type* of employment. This determines your taxes, your rights, and your job security.

Staffing Agencies vs. Direct Hire

Most immigrants get their first "survival" job through a *staffing agency* (also called a temp agency).

- **How it works:** You work for the agency, but you perform the work at another company (the "client").
- **The benefit:** It is the fastest way to get a paycheck. They often hire with minimal local experience.
- **The risk:** You can be let go at any time without notice. Use this as a stepping stone but always keep looking for a permanent and direct-hire role.

Hourly vs. Salary

- **Hourly pay:** You are paid for every minute you work. If you work more than 40 hours a week, you are usually entitled to *overtime pay* (often 1.5x your normal rate). This is common for survival jobs. (Check with your State or province for overtime law).
- **Salaried:** You are paid a fixed amount per year, regardless of whether you work 35 or 50 hours a week. This is more common in professional office jobs.

Exempt vs. Non-Exempt (The Overtime Rule)

This is a technical term that surprises many newcomers:

- **Non-exempt:** You are *not* exempt from overtime laws. The company *must* pay you extra if you work extra. (Most survival jobs are here).
- **Exempt:** You are exempt from overtime pay. No matter how much you work, your paycheck stays the same.

Employee (W-2/T4) vs. Independent Contractor (1099/T4A slip)

This is the most dangerous area for newcomers.

- **W-2 (US) and T4 (Canada):** You are a standard employee. The company handles your taxes and pays into your social security/pension. This is the safest for newcomers.
- **1099/T4A slip (contractor / self-employed worker):** The company pays you the gross amount without taxes withheld, and *you are responsible for saving your own taxes and eventually for your retirement.* Many newcomers spend the whole check, only to realize at the end of the year they owe thousands of dollars to the government.

💡 Pro Tip: The 30% Rule

If you are hired as an independent contractor, immediately put *30% of every check* into a separate savings account. That money belongs to the government, not you.

The "Job Offer" Comparison Table

Feature	Hourly (Non-Exempt)	Salary (Exempt)	Independent Contractor
Overtime Pay	Yes (1.5x)	Usually No	No
Tax Withheld	Yes (Company does it)	Yes (Company does it)	No (You must do it)
Benefits	Sometimes	Usually	None
Security	Moderate	High	Low

The Anatomy of a Paycheck: Gross vs. Net

When you look at your pay stub, you will see two main numbers.

- **Gross pay:** The total amount you earned before any deductions (hours worked times hourly rate).
- **Net pay (take-home pay):** The actual amount of the check or the direct deposit to your bank account.

Common Deductions (Where the money goes):

- **Federal Income Tax** — Your contribution to the national government.

- **State/Provincial Income Tax** —Your contribution to local services like roads and schools.
- **FICA / CPP & EI** — In the US, FICA goes toward Social Security (retirement) and Medicare. In Canada, CPP (Pension) and EI (Employment Insurance) are deducted.
- **Health Insurance** — If your company provides medical coverage, your portion of the premium (the cost of the insurance) is taken out here.

First Paycheck Vocabulary

Keep this list handy when you open your first pay stub.

- **YTD (Year-to-Date):** The total amount you have earned/paid in taxes from January 1 through this stub.
- **Direct Deposit:** The electronic transfer of your net pay directly into your bank account. (Highly recommended over paper checks!)
- **Withholding:** The amount of money your employer holds back to pay the government on your behalf.
- **Pay Period:** The timeframe you are being paid for (usually weekly, bi-weekly, or monthly).

💡 Pro Tip: The Tax Refund Secret

If you arrive midway through the year, you might have too much tax withheld from your checks because the system assumes you worked the whole year. When you file your taxes the following spring, you will likely get a *tax refund*, a lump sum of money sent back to you by the government. Think of it as a forced savings account for your first year!

The Bridge to Your Professional Future (Credential Recognition)

While you are working your survival job, your professional identity is not "on hold." It is in transition. In North America, your degree or certification from home usually needs a "translation" into the local system. This is called **Educational Credential Assessment (ECA)**.

Why do this now? Evaluation can take two to six months. If you start while working your survival job, your paperwork will be ready when you are financially stable enough to apply for professional roles.

The Three Steps to Reclaiming Your Career:

1. **Identify the Evaluator.** Most employers and licensing boards use third-party services like WES (World Education Services), ECE (Educational Credential Evaluators) or ICAS (International Credential Assessment Service of Canada). Check the specific requirements for your province or state.
2. **Request Official Transcripts.** This is often the hardest part. You usually need your university back home to send your records *directly* to the evaluation agency. Start this process early, as international mail and university administrations can be slow.

3. **The "Equivalency" Result:** You will receive a report stating that your degree is equivalent to a North American bachelor's or master's degree, or doctorate. This report is your *professional passport.*

💡 Pro Tip: Don't Go Back to School (Yet!)

Many newcomers assume they need to "start over" and get a new degree. This is often an expensive mistake. *Evaluate first.* You might find that you only need one or two local "bridge" courses to be fully licensed, saving you thousands of dollars and years of time.

🛠 The Employment Toolkit

Tool: The Job Application Funnel

Applying for jobs is a numbers game. To get one "yes" you often need five interviews. To get five interviews, you need fifty applications.

- Top of the funnel: 40+ Applications per week (Indeed, LinkedIn, ZipRecruiter)
- Middle of the funnel: 5–10 follow-up calls or walk-ins
- Bottom of the funnel: 1 solid job offer

Tool: The "Walk-In" Script

Sometimes, a smile and a handshake beat an online algorithm. Print ten resumes, dress neatly, and visit local businesses between 2:00 PM and 4:00 PM (when they aren't busy).

What to say: *"Hello, my name is [Name]. I recently moved to the area and I'm looking for work. I'm hardworking and available to start immediately. May I leave a resume with the manager?"*

Tool: The Local-Ready Resume Template

Entry-level hiring managers spend about *six seconds* looking at a resume. Use this simple structure to ensure yours passes the test.

- **Header:** Include name, local phone number, and professional email address.
- **Availability (the most important part):** State clearly, "Available 40+ hours/week, including weekends and evenings."
- **Core Skills:** List 4–5 things you are good at (e.g., cash handling, heavy lifting, punctuality, customer service).
- **Work History:** List your last 2–3 jobs. Focus on *what you did* (e.g., "Managed inventory for a busy shop," and "Provided childcare for 3 families").
- **Education:** Keep it brief. If you have a degree from home, list it, but don't let it overshadow your current skills.

Tool: The Application Volume Tracker

Applying for jobs can feel discouraging if you don't see the numbers. Use this tracker to stay disciplined. If you haven't secured a job, your goal is to fill all slots every single day.

Date	Company	Role	How I Applied	Follow-up Date

Tool: The "Interview Cheat Sheet"

Before you walk into an interview, memorize these three *value statements*. They work for almost any entry-level role.

- **Reliability Statement**: "In my previous roles, I was never late. I understand that the team depends on me to be here on time, every time."
- **Learning Statement**: "I am a fast learner. If you show me the system once, I will work hard to master it by the end of my first shift."
- **Flexibility Statement**: "I am focused on building my new life here, so I am very flexible with my schedule and can pick up extra shifts as needed."

Tool: Professional Transition Checklist

Use this list to track your progress toward your "dream job" while you work your "survival job."

- ☐ **Gather Documents:** Do you have your original diplomas and transcripts in a safe, waterproof folder?
- ☐ **Certified Translation:** If your documents are not in English (and French for Canada), have you found a certified translator? (Do not translate them yourself; they won't be accepted.)
- ☐ **Select an Agency:** Have you researched whether WES (World Education Services), ICAS (International Credential Assessment Service of Canada) ECE (Educational Credential Evaluators), or a specific professional board (like an engineering or nursing board) is required for your field?
- ☐ **Bridge Fund:** Have you set aside $200–$400 in your stability fund specifically for evaluation fees?

- ☐ **Update Your LinkedIn:** Have you changed your LinkedIn location to your new city and listed your foreign degree using the North American equivalent title?

Real-Life Illustration: The "Afternoon Walk"

I remember David, an immigrant from the Congo with no local contacts who applied for fifty jobs online and heard nothing. He was getting desperate. I told him to print ten resumes and walk down the main street of his neighborhood.

At the fourth shop, a small hardware store, the manager was frustrated because a worker had just quit. David walked in, smiled, and handed over his resume. The manager didn't even look at his past experience or care about David's accent; he looked at his punctuality, determination, and presence. David started the next morning.

The Lesson: The internet is great, but your determination and humility is your strongest asset in the first 30 days.

Real-Life Illustration: The Paycheck That Changed Everything

The first job I got wasn't in my field, and the uniform and the environment were a bit uncomfortable. But I will never forget the feeling of holding that first paycheck. It was more than just paper; it was proof that *I belonged here, that I could take care of my kids. It put me back in charge.* I stopped panicking when I walked into the grocery store. I stopped feeling like a guest and started feeling like a resident. That first "survival job" gave me the mental peace I needed to eventually move back to the career I actually wanted. *Hustle now so you can choose later.*

Chapter Reflection

1. **Is my pride in the way?** Am I avoiding certain jobs because of what people back home might think? (Remember: They aren't the ones paying your rent.)
2. **Am I playing the numbers?** Have I applied to enough places today to realistically expect a "yes"?
3. **What are my "yes" criteria?** In the first 30 days, the "perfect" job is the one that says, "You're hired."

Action Steps: The 14-Day Mission

- ☐ **Days 1–2:** Create a simple one-page resume. Set up profiles on Indeed and LinkedIn.
- ☐ **Days 3–7:** The Volume Phase. Apply for ten jobs every single day.
- ☐ **Days 8–10:** The Footwork Phase. Walk into five local businesses and ask for the manager.
- ☐ **Days 11–14:** The Selection Phase. Go to every interview you are offered. Accept the first offer that provides steady hours and safe conditions.

CHAPTER 7

The Mindset of a New Immigrant — Confidence, Discipline, and Patience

Let me tell you a truth that many newcomers only realize after months of unnecessary struggle: Your mind is your first home in this new country. Before the apartment, before the paycheck, and before the bank account, your mindset is the engine that determines how far you will go. You may arrive with very little, but if your mindset is strong, this country will open doors for you. Conversely, you may arrive with money and degrees, but if your mindset is weak, the challenges of relocation will humble you.

Let's build the inner strength that will protect you, lift you, and guide you through the first 90 days.

The Three Pillars of the Immigrant Spirit

1. Confidence: The Courage to Be a Beginner

Confidence is not pretending you know everything. It is quietly believing that you can **figure things out**.

- You don't need perfect English to succeed today.
- You don't need to understand every complex rule on day one.
- Believe in your ability to adapt. Confidence is the courage to ask a "silly" question or take a bus in the wrong direction and simply try again.

2. Discipline: Your Greatest Competitive Advantage

In life, luck is rare; discipline is reliable. In the first 90 days, discipline is what separates those who stabilize from those who spiral.

- Discipline is waking up early for a long commute, saving money when your peers are spending, and showing up to work with a positive attitude even when you are tired.
- Discipline leads employers to trust you and helps you climb *from survival work to career growth*.

3. Patience: The Timeline of Truth

Many immigrants arrive with "instant success" expectations. But meaningful progress is a slow cooker, not a microwave.

- Understand the timeline: realize that month one is for survival.
- If you are safe and fed, you are winning. Breakthroughs usually happen in years, not weeks.

Navigating the Cultural "Operating System"

To succeed in North America, you must understand the local unwritten rules.

- **Time is currency:** Being five minutes early is considered on time. Being exactly on time is considered late.
- **Direct communication:** People value clarity. If you don't understand an instruction, say: "Could you please explain that again? I want to make sure I do it correctly."
- **The Initiative Rule:** Don't wait to be told what to do. Managers love employees who ask, "What else can I help with?"

🛠 The Mindset Toolkit

Tool: The Purpose Statement Card

When the days get hard (and they will), you need to remember *why* you are here.

Action: Write a one-sentence purpose statement on a piece of paper and keep it in your wallet. Examples: *"I am working this job today so that my children can have a better education tomorrow." "I am disciplined today so I can be free in three years."*

Tool: "Circle of Control" Exercise

Anxiety comes from trying to control things you can't. Use this mental filter daily:

Things I CANNOT Control	Things I CAN Control
The weather — The economy	My attitude and effort at work
How long the government takes to mail my ID	How many jobs I apply for today
What people back home think of me	How I manage my $50 grocery budget

Tool: The Daily Wins Tracker

Success in the first 90 days is rarely about big promotions; it is about small, consistent victories. Use this simple log to train your brain to see progress, even on hard days. For example:

Date	The Small Win	Why it Matters
Jan 15	I asked a bus driver for directions.	I am overcoming my fear of speaking.
Jan 16	I saved $10 by packing my lunch.	I am practicing financial discipline.
Jan 17	I finished my shift with a smile.	I am building a local reputation for reliability.

Tool: The Immigrant Growth Timeline

Use this visual guide to manage your expectations. When you feel frustrated, look at where you are in the cycle. Most people quit because they expect year three results in month two.

- **Months 1–3 (Survival):** High stress, low income, high learning curve. **Goal: Stability.**
- **Months 4–12 (Stability):** Steady job, small savings, understanding the system. **Goal: Consistency.**
- **Years 1–3 (Growth):** Career advancement, better housing, building credit. **Goal: Upward mobility.**

Tool: The "Resilience" Morning Routine

Discipline starts in the first ten minutes of your day. Before you check your phone or look at social media, complete these three "warrior tasks."

1. **Hydration hit:** Drink a full glass of water (physical readiness).
2. **Purpose statement:** Say out loud: "I am here to build a future, and today's work is the foundation."
3. **Priority one:** Identify the *one* most important task for today (e.g., "Hand in the apartment application" or "Ask for extra hours at work").

Real-Life Illustration: The Two Neighbors

I once knew two men, Yusuf and Anton, who arrived at the same time and lived in the same building.

Yusuf spent his time complaining about how difficult the buses were and how the weather was too cold. He felt shame about working in a kitchen and stayed home whenever he felt sad. After 90 days, he was still struggling to pay rent.

Anton decided that every bus ride was a language lesson. He wore two sweaters to stay warm and arrived at his cleaning job ten minutes early every day. He told himself, "This mop is the key to my first house." By month six, Anton's manager promoted him to a supervisor because of his *discipline.*

Yusuf was still waiting for "luck" to find him. The country didn't treat them differently; their mindsets did.

Real-Life Illustration: The Warrior's Secret

Let me share something raw. Many of the most successful immigrants you see today—the business owners, the doctors, the homeowners—cried in secret during their first 90 days. They cried in bus station bathrooms, on late-night shifts, and into their pillows at night.

Starting over is emotional. Leaving your mother, your father, or your children hurts. But do you know what makes them warriors? *They wiped their tears, got up, and went to work anyway.* They didn't let their emotions drive the car; they let their discipline do the steering. You are not weak for feeling overwhelmed; you are becoming a warrior through the process.

Chapter Reflection

Take a deep breath and be honest with yourself.

1. **Am I comparing my chapter 1 to someone else's chapter 20?** Stop looking at social media; focus on your own feet.
2. **Is my pride protecting me or is it a prison?** Am I refusing a survival job because of a title I had back home?

3. **What was my small win today**—even if it was just learning a new English word or finding a cheaper grocery store?

Action Steps: Mindset Maintenance

- ☐ **Daily Purpose Check:** Read your "purpose statement" every morning before you leave the house.
- ☐ **The "No-Comparison" Fast:** For the next 30 days, avoid looking at the social media profiles of people who make you feel behind.
- ☐ **One New Fact:** Learn one new thing about the local system or culture every single day.
- ☐ **Physical Pride:** Even if you live in a tiny room, keep it perfectly clean. Discipline in your space leads to discipline in your finances.

CHAPTER 8

Workplace Etiquette — Understanding the Culture

Securing your first job is a major victory, but keeping it and growing within it requires a new set of skills. In North America, many immigrants lose opportunities not because they lack technical ability but because they unintentionally clash with *workplace culture.*

This chapter is your guide to navigating these unwritten rules. These expectations are not about changing who you are; they are about understanding the values of the environment you've joined so you can thrive within it.

Time is King: The Rule of Punctuality

In the US and Canada, being on time isn't just a suggestion; it is a sign of respect.

- **The Early Rule:** Arriving five to ten minutes before your shift starts is considered on time. Arriving exactly at your start time is often seen as being behind.
- **Break Discipline:** If you have a thirty-minute lunch, be back at your station at minute thirty.
- **Communication:** If an emergency makes you late, call or text your supervisor immediately. Do not just show up late with an explanation.
- **The Logic:** To an employer, *Late = Unreliable.*

Mastering the Social Code — Small Talk and Culture

In many cultures, you go to work strictly to work. In North America, workplace relationships are built in the "in-between" moments—at the coffee machine, in the elevator, or in the three minutes before a meeting starts. This is called *small talk.*

Small talk feels like a waste of time, but it's actually a safety check. It shows your coworkers that you are friendly, approachable, and part of the team. People hire and promote those they *like* working with.

"Safe" Topics (The Big Three)

If you aren't sure what to say, stick to these three "safe" zones:

- **The Weather:** "It's freezing today, isn't it?" "I hope it clears up for the weekend."
- **The Weekend:** On Monday, "How was your weekend? Did you do anything fun?" On Friday, "Any big plans for the weekend?"

- **Local Sports:** Even if you don't play, knowing if the local team won or lost gives you an instant connection.

Topics to Avoid (The Danger Zone)

To stay professional, never discuss these three things at work unless you know someone very well:

- **Politics:** It is highly divisive and can create enemies.
- **Religion:** Keep your faith private in the professional sphere.
- **Money/Salary:** Asking a coworker how much they earn is considered very rude in North American culture.

The Coffee Break Script

Use these openers to start a conversation without feeling awkward.

- **Observation:** "I notice you have a [team name/brand] mug. Are you a fan?"
- **Newcomer Honesty:** "I'm still exploring the city. Do you have a favorite place to get lunch around here?"
- **Work-Related:** "That was a great point you made in the meeting. How long have you been working on this project?"

Pro Tip: The "Direct" Feedback Rule

In North America, bosses often use a "feedback sandwich." They say something good, then a correction (the bad news), then something good again.

- **Feedback sandwich:** "You're doing great with customers [good], but you need to be faster with the paperwork [correction]. Keep up the high energy! [good]"
- **The Lesson:** Don't ignore the middle part! That correction is the most important part of the conversation.

Communication: Direct and Professional

In many cultures, politeness involves being indirect. In North America, *clarity is more important than "beating around the bush."*

- **Be Specific.** Instead of saying, "I might be able to help on Saturday if things work out," say, "Yes, I am available on Saturday" or "No, I cannot work Saturday, but I am available Sunday."
- **Ask Questions:** If you don't understand an instruction, it is better to ask for clarification than to guess and make a mistake. Employers value the honesty of: "I'm not sure how to do that yet. Can you show me one more time?"

Boundaries and Personal Space

North Americans value "the bubble"—a physical and emotional distance in the workplace.

- **Physical Space:** Maintain about an arm's length of distance when speaking to someone. Avoid casual touching (like a hand on a shoulder).
- **Professional Privacy:** Avoid asking coworkers personal questions about their salary, religion, or family problems early on. Keep the conversation focused on work or light topics like the weather and hobbies.

Safety and Rules: The "Why" Behind the Policy

Companies here are legally responsible for your safety. When they insist on safety gear or specific procedures, it isn't just about being strict—it's about protection. Ignoring a safety rule is often grounds for immediate termination. *Follow the manual to the letter.*

Professionalism vs. Friendship

Your coworkers may be very friendly, but don't confuse work friends with family.

- **The Reality:** People often keep their work and private lives completely separate.
- **The Strategy:** Be kind and helpful to everyone, but don't take it personally if you aren't invited to personal gatherings right away. Focus on being a great *teammate* first.

Final Words: Mastering workplace etiquette isn't about hiding your heritage; it's about adding a professional layer to your skills. When you respect the local clock and the local boundaries, you become a person that everyone wants to hire and promote.

🛠 The Workplace Toolkit

Tool: "Initiative" Checklist

Managers look for people who "see the work" without being told. Use this checklist when you have a slow moment:

- ☐ **Clean:** Is my area organized?
- ☐ **Assist:** Does a coworker look overwhelmed?
- ☐ **Prepare:** Am I ready for the next hour's tasks?
- ☐ **The Magic Question:** Ask your boss, "I've finished my tasks; is there anything else I can help with?"

Tool: The Feedback Filter

Feedback can feel like an attack on your character, but in this culture, it is a **tool for growth**.

When you hear:	It actually means:	The Best Response:
"You're doing this wrong."	"I want you to be efficient."	"Thank you for showing me. I'll do it this way now."
"You need to work faster."	"The team is falling behind."	"I understand. I'll focus on increasing my speed."
"Can we talk about your tardiness?"	"I need to rely on you."	"I apologize. I will adjust my commute to ensure I'm early."

Tool: Transit Etiquette Guide

Blending into your new community starts on the bus or train.

- **The "Silent" Rule:** North Americans generally prefer a quiet commute. Avoid playing music out loud or having loud phone conversations. Always use headphones.
- **Exit Strategy:** On a crowded bus, move toward the rear door before your stop. Simply say "excuse me" to get past others; there is no need for long explanations.
- **Priority Seating:** Always give up your seat for the elderly, pregnant women, and people with disabilities. It is often the law, and it marks you as a respectful member of society.

Real-Life Illustration: The 15-Minute Turnaround

I met a newcomer who was a brilliant mechanic. However, he arrived fifteen minutes late twice in his first week at work. When his manager confronted him, the mechanic felt insulted. "In my country, we care about the quality of the work, not the clock!" he thought.

Thankfully, a mentor pulled him aside and explained: "The manager thinks if you don't respect his time, you won't respect his tools or his customers." The mechanic shifted his mindset. He started arriving ten minutes early every day. Within three months, he was the most trusted person in the shop. *The quality of your work gets you the job; your respect for the culture gets you the promotion.*

Chapter Reflection

1. **Am I listening to understand or listening to defend?** When someone corrects me, is my first instinct to argue?
2. **Is my "work voice" professional?** Am I avoiding gossip and keeping my tone calm even when I'm stressed?
3. **Am I a "solution finder"?** When I see a problem, do I bring it to my boss with a possible solution, or with a complaint?

Action Plan: Mastering the Culture

- ☐ **The 5-Minute Rule:** For the next week, commit to being at your workspace five minutes before your shift starts.
- ☐ **The Notes Habit:** Carry a small notebook. When a supervisor gives instructions, write them down. It shows you are serious and prevents mistakes.
- ☐ **The Feedback Challenge:** This week, ask your supervisor: "How am I doing so far? Is there anything I can improve?" This shows incredible maturity.
- ☐ **Organize Your Space:** Spend the last five minutes of every shift cleaning your area. It leaves a lasting impression of discipline.

CHAPTER 9

Healthcare — Protecting Your Body and Your Bank Account

For many immigrants, healthcare back home was either free or so inexpensive that you didn't think twice about it. In North America, healthcare is high-stakes financial issue. If you treat it with your home country mindset, you are one accident away from bankruptcy.

The Insurance Safety Net

If you qualify for government-funded healthcare, apply as soon as you arrive. In the United States, low-income immigrants may be eligible for Medicaid, which provides free or low-cost medical coverage depending on your status and your state. In Canada, newcomers qualify for provincial health insurance, but some provinces require a waiting period of up to 90 days, so apply for your health card immediately and consider temporary private insurance. Understanding your eligibility early protects your Fortress Fund from unexpected medical bills.

In the US, medical debt is the #1 cause of personal bankruptcy. In Canada, while doctors are "free," prescriptions, dental, and vision are not.

- **Employer bridge:** Most professional jobs offer health benefits. When evaluating a job offer, a $60k salary with full benefits is often better than a $65k salary with none.
- **Gap trap:** If you are between jobs, never go uninsured. Look into COBRA (US) or provincial programs (Canada) to ensure you have a safety net of coverage.

The "Hidden" Costs: Dental and Vision

You might think you can "tough it out," but a tooth infection can cost $3,000 in an emergency room, whereas a $100 cleaning might have prevented the infection entirely.

The Strategy: Use your Fortress Fund for preventative care. It is cheaper to maintain your health than to repair it.

Understanding "In-Network" vs. "Out-of-Network" (US-Specific)

The most common health insurance mistake immigrants make in the US is going to the nearest hospital without checking if their insurance covers it.

The Rule: Know where your "in-network" urgent care is located before you are sick.

Decoding the Insurance Dialect

Think of health insurance not as a free pass but as a *partnership* between you and the insurance provider. You both pay a share of the costs.

Important Note for Newcomers: Many employers have a *90-day waiting period* before you can join the company plan. During these first three months, you are in the "exposure zone." If you are currently in this window, read this section now to understand the system, then *set a calendar reminder* to return to this page the day your eligibility begins. Since this is our only deep dive into healthcare in this three-book series, treat it as your permanent reference guide.

The Four Key Terms You Must Know:

- **Premium:** This is the "membership fee." It is the amount taken out of your paycheck (or paid monthly) just to have the insurance active. You pay this even if you never see a doctor.
- **Deductible:** This is the amount you must pay out of pocket for certain medical services *before* your insurance begins sharing the cost. However, **not every service requires you to meet the deductible first**. Many plans allow you to pay only a **copay** for doctor visits, urgent care, or even emergency room visits, *even if your deductible has not been met.*
- **Strategic Note:** If your plan has a $2,000 deductible, it's wise to keep that amount in your Fortress Fund, because services that *do* apply to the deductible (like MRIs, some tests, or hospital bills) will require you to pay the full allowed amount until the deductible is met.
- **Copay / Coinsurance:** A **copay** is a fixed fee (for example, $30 for a doctor visit or $250 for an ER visit). A **coinsurance** is a percentage you pay (for example, you pay 20% and insurance pays 80%) *after* you've met your deductible. Importantly, **many routine services only require a copay and do not require you**

to pay your deductible first, depending on your plan and whether the provider is in network.

- **Out-of-Pocket Maximum:** This is your "safety ceiling." This is the most you will *ever* have to pay in a single year. Once you hit this number, the insurance company pays 100% of everything else. This is what prevents a massive hospital stay from becoming a life-long debt.

🛠 The Healthcare Toolkit

Tool: Worst-Case Scenario Planner

Use this to ensure your Fortress Fund is deep enough. Once your benefits begin, look at your insurance plan and fill in these numbers.

	Number	**Impact on your Savings**
Individual Deductible	$_______	Cash you need ready in your Fortress Fund
Out-of-Pocket Max	$_______	The worst-case cost of a major accident
ER Copay	$_______	The cost of a single midnight emergency visit

The Strategist's Rule: Your Fortress Fund should ideally equal your deductible + $1,000. This ensures that a medical event doesn't force you into high-interest credit card debt.

Tool: Healthcare Navigator Matrix

Use this to decide where to go when you or your family feels unwell. Choosing the wrong door can cost you thousands.

Where to Go	When to Use It	Estimated Cost	Impact on Fortress Fund
Primary Doctor	Checkups, cold/flu, ongoing issues	Low (usually a copay)	Minimal — often does not touch your deductible
Urgent Care	Stitches, minor fractures, infections	Moderate (copay + possible coinsurance)	Manageable — some services may apply to deductible
Emergency Room	Life threatening issues, chest pain, major trauma	Very High (ER copay + services)	Significant — can quickly use up your deductible
Pharmacy / Telehealth	Refills, minor rashes, quick advice	Very Low (small copay or free)	None — rarely affects deductible

Real-Life Illustration: The High-Deductible Trap

Let's look at Omar. He chose a "cheap" insurance plan because the monthly premium was only $50. However, the plan had a *$5,000 deductible.*

- **The Incident:** Omar broke his arm playing soccer. The hospital bill was $4,500.
- **The Result:** Because the bill was *less* than his deductible, the insurance company paid *$0*. Omar had to use his entire Fortress Fund and take a loan to pay the hospital.
- **The Lesson:** A "cheap" plan is often the most expensive for a newcomer with low savings. Sometimes, paying a higher monthly premium for a *lower deductible* is the smarter move in your first two years.

Real-Life Illustration: The "Emergency" Choice

Let's look at Sam and Yara. Both have a high fever on a Saturday night.

- **Sam (The Reactive):** Panics and goes straight to the Emergency Room (ER). He waits six hours and receives a bill for $2,500 because it wasn't a life-threatening emergency. His savings are gone.
- **Yara (The Strategic):** Checks her insurance app. She finds an "in-network" Urgent Care open until midnight. She is seen in thirty minutes and pays a $50 copay.

The Result: Yara saved $2,450 by knowing how to navigate the system.

Chapter Reflection

1. **Do I understand how my insurance works, or am I avoiding it because it feels confusing?** When a medical issue comes up, will I know which place to go first?
2. **Am I protecting my Fortress Fund?** Have I set aside enough to cover my deductible and unexpected copays, or am I hoping emergencies won't happen?
3. **When I feel unwell, do I pause and choose the right door — primary care, urgent care, ER, or telehealth — or do I act out of fear or habit?** Each choice affects both my health and my wallet.

Action Steps: Healthcare Audit

1. **Check Your Eligibility Date:** If you just started your job, ask HR: "When is the exact date my health coverage begins?" Mark it on your calendar.
2. **Find Your Portal:** Log into your employer's health insurance portal. Find your "Summary of Benefits." Also look for your deductible and out-of-pocket maximum. Print these out.
3. **Cover the Vulnerable Period:** If you are in your first 90 days and have no coverage, avoid high-risk activities (like contact sports), and research visitor insurance or short-term health plans to cover catastrophic accidents.
4. **Fortress Fund Check:** Once insured, does your Fortress Fund have enough to cover your deductible? If not, start or increase your autodeposit savings until that gap is closed.
5. **HSA/FSA Advantage**: Ask your HR department if they offer a Health Savings Account (HSA) or Flexible Savings Account (FSA). These allow you to save for your deductible using pre-tax money, meaning the government essentially gives you a 20% discount on your healthcare.
6. **Map Your Network**: Find the nearest in-network urgent care and pharmacy. Put their addresses in your phone's emergency contacts.
7. **Wellness Check**: Schedule one dental cleaning this month. Preventative care is a financial strategy.

CHAPTER 10

Your 90-Day Action Plan — The Roadmap to Stability

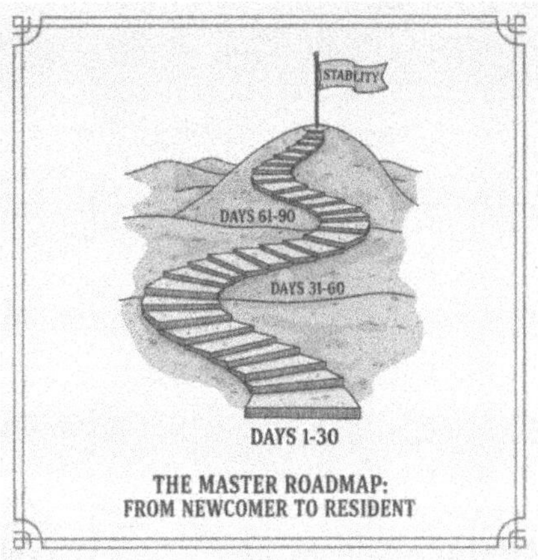

THE MASTER ROADMAP:
FROM NEWCOMER TO RESIDENT

The first 90 days in a new country are the most critical. This window of time determines whether you will struggle for years or build a foundation that supports you for a lifetime.

This chapter is your **Master Roadmap**. It consolidates everything we've discussed into a clear, achievable timeline. Think of this not as a list of chores, but as a series of milestones that lead you from being a newcomer to becoming a *stable resident*.

Phase 1 — Days 1 to 30: The Survival and Setup Phase

Your Mission: Secure your identity, protect your cash, and find your first foothold.

Key Milestones

- **Identity Lockdown:** Apply for your SSN/SIN and State/Provincial ID immediately. These are the keys that unlock every other door.
- **Financial Fortification:** Open checking and savings accounts. Move your cash into the bank to protect it from loss and theft.
- **Survival Job:** Secure *any* safe, legal income within the first 21 days. Don't wait for the "perfect" role; wait for the first "yes."
- **Transit Mastery:** Learn the bus and train routes between your housing, the grocery store, and industrial/retail hubs where jobs are located.

Phase 1 Checklist

- ☐ Applied for SSN/SIN. (Keep the receipt!)
- ☐ Opened bank accounts and activated mobile banking.
- ☐ Created a Four Walls budget (Food, Shelter, Transportation, Communications).
- ☐ Applied for 10–20 jobs daily.
- ☐ Secured a local SIM card and phone plan.

Phase 2 — Days 31 to 60: The Momentum and Stability Phase

Your Mission: Move from *panic* to *process*. Establish a routine and start saving.

Key Milestones

- **Workplace Integration:** At your first job, focus on being the most reliable person. Learn the unwritten rules of North American workplace etiquette (punctuality and directness).
- **Savings Seed:** Aim to save your first **$500**. This is your Sleep Well at Night fund.
- **Housing Research:** Start visiting neighborhoods. If you are staying with friends, set a target date to move into your own room or studio.
- **Knowledge Test:** Study the driver's manual and pass your written exam. Even if you don't have a car yet, having the permit is progress.

Phase 2 Checklist

- ☐ Received first full month of paychecks.
- ☐ Reached $500 in savings.
- ☐ Passed the written driver's test.
- ☐ Identified three safe neighborhoods for long-term housing.
- ☐ Tracked every dollar spent for 30 days.

Phase 3 — Days 61 to 90: The Foundation and Future Phase

Your Mission: Move from *stability* to *permanence*. Secure your own space and look ahead.

Key Milestones

- **Lease:** Most successful newcomers move into semipermanent housing (a studio, shared apartment, or room) during this third month. Sign a lease that is no more than 30–35% of your monthly income.

- **System Optimization:** Set up autopay for your phone and utility bills to ensure you never miss a payment. This protects your future credit.
- **Career Assessment:** Now that you have a job and a home, ask yourself: *What certifications or training do I need to move from this survival job into my actual career?*
- **Reputation Check:** By day 90, you should have at least one local professional reference: a manager or coworker who can vouch for your hard work.

Phase 3 Checklist

- ☐ Signed a rental agreement or lease.
- ☐ Moved into long-term housing.
- ☐ Established a weekly "Money Minute" — a 10–15-minute check-in to review your budget, track spending, and make sure you're staying on plan.
- ☐ Maintained a clean bank record (no overdrafts or hidden fees).
- ☐ Identified the *next step* job or certification for the coming year.

🛠 The 90-Day Master Toolkit

Tool: Success-at-a-Glance Timeline

Use this visual overview to track your progress. If you get stuck on a Phase 1 task in Month 2, don't panic, just refocus and finish it.

Phase	Focus	Emotional State
Days 1–30	**Logistics** (ID, bank, job 1)	High Stress — High Energy
Days 31–60	**Habits** (savings, commute, culture)	Fatigue — Determination
Days 61–90	**Roots** (housing, health care, credit prep, planning)	Relief — Growing Confidence

Tool: The Emergency Exit Plan

What happens if you lose your job or an unexpected bill arrives?

The Rule: If your savings drop below $200, immediately revert to *ultra-survival mode*: no eating out, no data-heavy streaming, and double your job applications. Having a plan for bad days prevents them from becoming *bad months.*

Real-Life Illustration: 90-Day Transformation

Let's talk about two friends, Carlos and Jean, from Benin and Ivory Coast respectively.

The "Vacation" Trap: For the first 30 days, Carlos felt like he was on a holiday. He spent his time visiting sights, enjoying the city, and relaxing, thinking he had plenty of time to find work later. By day 60, however, the reality set in: he was almost out of cash. Desperate and panicked, he took the very first job he could find, a position that paid poorly and treated him badly.

The "90-Day Plan" Approach: Jean did things differently. He adopted the 90-day plan. While Carlos was touring, Jean was in library computer labs, attending networking events, and knocking on office doors. By day 60, because he was focused, Jean had already saved $800 and secured a steady job at a warehouse. On day 85, Jean signed a lease for a small, clean studio apartment that he could afford on his own.

Day 90—The Coffee Shop: When they met for coffee on day 90, the difference was obvious. Carlos looked exhausted, defeated, and worried about his next paycheck. Jean was tired—after all, he had worked harder than ever—but his eyes were bright with hope. He looked at Carlos and said, "The first 90 days were the hardest work of my life, *but today, I finally feel like I live here.*"

Chapter Reflection

- **Am I clear about which phase of the newcomer timeline I'm in, or am I trying to jump ahead too quickly?** Am I reaching for Phase 3 goals — like finding a dream home — while still completing the essentials of Phase 1, such as securing ID and a first job?
- **Am I willing to take a small starter job for now, knowing it can open the door to a bigger, more stable life later**? Am I choosing progress over pride?
- **What is one thing I've done in the last 90 days that makes me genuinely proud of my journey so far?** Even small wins matter — they are signs of momentum.

Action Steps: The Next 90 Days

Your first 90 days were about *survival*. Your next 90 days will be about *growth*.

- ☐ Review your *purpose statement* from chapter 7.
- ☐ Print out the 90-Day Stability Cheat Sheet below and check off the boxes as you go.
- ☐ Once you're ready, start book 2, where we will master the **credit system, career advancement, and wealth building.**

Final Words: My friend, you have done what millions are too afraid to do. You have changed your country and started from zero. If you have made it to day 90, *you have already won.* You are no longer just a newcomer; you are a builder. Keep building.

The 90-Day Stability Cheat Sheet

Keep this page on your fridge or save a photo of it on your phone. These are your non-negotiables.

Phase 1: Survival (Days 1–30)

- ☐ **Secure identity:** Get your SSN/SIN and State/Provincial ID immediately. Without these, you don't "exist" in the system.
- ☐ **Protect the Four Walls:** Prioritize spending on **food, shelter, basic transit, and phone**. Everything else is a luxury.
- ☐ **Open a bank account:** Move your cash into a secure, insured account. Set up autopay for your phone bill to start protecting your future credit.
- ☐ **Learn the map:** Download a transit app (Moovit/Google Maps) and learn the bus routes to the grocery store and the library.

Phase 2: Stabilization (Days 31–60)

☐ **Get the "Survival Job":** Don't wait for the perfect job. Secure a paycheck now to stop bleeding your savings.

☐ **The Three-Quote Rule:** If you are buying insurance or a phone plan, never take the first offer. Compare at least three.

☐ **Inspect before buying:** If buying a used car, a mechanic's inspection is mandatory. No exceptions.

☐ **Know your rights:** Your landlord must give notice (24 hours) to enter, and utilities like heat and water are often included in the rent, though in some locations they must be paid separately.

Phase 3: Building (Days 61–90)

☐ **Evaluate your credentials:** If you have credentials to transfer, start the WES/ICAS/ ECE process. Send your transcripts for evaluation so your professional bridge is ready.

☐ **Master the social code:** Practice small talk at work. Be on time (five minutes early). Listen for the Feedback Sandwich.

☐ **Secured credit:** Ask your bank about a secured credit card to start building your score safely.

☐ **Look up:** Transition from Survival Mode to Strategy Mode. Update your LinkedIn and start networking in your professional field.

Emergency Quick-Dial List

9-1-1: Life-threatening emergencies only (police, fire, ambulance).

2-1-1: Essential community services (food banks, housing help, legal aid).

3-1-1: Non-emergency city services (trash, potholes, city info).

CHAPTER 11

Stories from the Journey — You Are Not Alone

Before we close this book, I want to pause and speak to you, not as a coach or a guide, but as someone who has stood exactly where you are standing.

Every immigrant carries a story inside them: a wound from what was left behind, a dream for what lies ahead, and a quiet, stubborn strength that refuses to give up. This chapter is dedicated to that story. Yours, mine, and the millions of others who have crossed oceans and borders to build something new.

When you understand that others have survived the same storm, you realize the storm is temporary, but your strength is permanent.

My Story: The Foundation of Zero

When I first arrived in North America from Cameroon, I had more ambition than money, and a *master's degree in information technology, backed by years of experience ranging from the private sector to supervising for the Ministry of Posts and Telecommunications.* Despite my credentials, I had no car, no credit, and no idea how cold the reality would feel. I spent my first weeks sleeping on a friend's couch, my clothes living in a plastic bin.

I took three buses and walked the last mile to get to my first temporary jobs. I did it all: security shifts, warehouse labor, grocery delivery, Amazon Flex, and driving for Uber/Lyft. I lifted boxes and cleaned rooms, not because I loved the work, but because every paycheck was a brick in my foundation, *desperately needed to support my new baby, raise my four children, and provide for the family back home who relied on me.*

Eventually, I *leveraged my background* to move into IT, gained expertise, bought a home, and started my own business.

The Lesson: Your beginning does not define your destiny. The struggle you feel today is the training ground for the success you will achieve tomorrow.

Marie's Story: The Power of Reliability

Marie arrived from Côte d'Ivoire as a single mother with a seven-year-old son and very basic English. Her first job was in a bakery, waking up at 3:45 a.m. to sweep floors and carry heavy trays.

Six months in, her supervisor said: *"You are the most reliable person on my team."* That one sentence changed her. She realized she wasn't just a newcomer; she was an asset. She took night classes, and five years later, she is a nursing assistant studying to become a registered nurse.

The Lesson: Reliability is a universal language. If you show up, you will eventually stand out.

José's Story: The Tool-by-Tool Strategy

José came from Guatemala with no connections. He started as a construction helper, doing the heavy-lifting work no one else wanted. But José had a secret plan:

- Every day, he learned **one** new English word.
- Every week, he saved **$20**.
- Every month, he bought **one** high-quality tool.

After two years, he was a licensed handyman. After four, he owned his own renovation business.

The Lesson: Small, disciplined investments in yourself compound into massive opportunities.

Aisha's Story: The Side-Door Entrance

Aisha was an accountant in Nigeria, but in her new home, every door was closed because she lacked local experience. Instead of giving up, she volunteered to do the books for a local community center.

That volunteer role led to a recommendation, which led to a small business job, which finally led to her current role as a senior financial analyst.

The Lesson: If the front door is locked, look for a side door. Experience is experience, whether it is for pay or volunteer.

Universal Truths of the Journey

Every story in this chapter is different, but they all share three immutable rules for success:

1. **Everyone starts at the bottom:** No one escapes the "starting over" phase. It is not a sign of failure; it is the first step of the climb.
2. **Consistency beats talent:** The strongest don't always win. The people who show up every single day, even when they are tired, are the ones who cross the finish line.
3. **Community is a catalyst:** Those who succeed are those who are brave enough to ask for help, join an association, or find a mentor.

🛠 The Success Identity Toolkit

Tool: Resilience Scale

When you feel like you are failing, use this scale to see how far you've actually come.

Phase	Milestone	Proof of Growth
Survival	I found a place to sleep and a way to eat.	I am resourceful.
Adjustment	I navigated the bus system and got an ID.	I am a fast learner.
Stability	I received my first paycheck and saved $10.	I am a builder.

Tool: Future Self Visualization

Close your eyes and imagine yourself five years from now. You are in your own home. You are driving a reliable car. You are helping a new immigrant who just arrived.

- **Action:** Write a short letter to that future you. Thank yourself for not giving up today. Keep this letter in your Power Folder.

Chapter Reflection

- **The Comparison Trap:** Am I looking at José or Marie's year five and feeling bad about my month one?
- **The Invisible Growth:** Can I see that even though my bank account is low, my knowledge of this country is 100% higher than it was the day I landed?
- **The Resilience Check:** If I survived the journey to get here, what makes me think I can't survive the journey to stay here?

Action Steps: Writing Your Next Page

- ☐ **Identify your "small win" of the week:** Did you learn a new route? Find a cheaper store? Write it down.
- ☐ **Find a success model:** Look for someone in your community who arrived five years ago and is doing well. Ask for ten minutes of their time to hear their story.
- ☐ **Practice quiet progress:** Today, do one thing that moves you forward without telling anyone about it. Let the result be your reward.

CHAPTER 12

From Survival to Stability

You are not behind. You are beginning. And beginnings are supposed to feel uncertain; that is where the growth happens. Ten years from now, you will look back and realize that these "hard days" were actually the days you became the strongest version of yourself.

Your story is powerful. Your dream is valid. *You are here, and that is the biggest victory of all.*

Congratulations! You have completed the first and most difficult leg of your journey. By reaching the end of this book, you've moved from the chaos of arrival to the structure of a plan.

To mark this milestone, here is your **book 1 Graduation Checklist**. This tool summarizes the essential "wins" you should have secured, or be working toward, before moving on to the advanced strategies of book 2.

Book 1: The First 90 Days Graduation Checklist

If you can check off these boxes, you have officially built a **Foundation of Stability.**

Section 1: The Essentials

- ☐ **Identity Key:** I have my SSN/SIN or at least the official receipt of application.
- ☐ **Daily ID:** I have a local State or Provincial photo ID.
- ☐ **Power Folder:** My passport, visa, and work permits are scanned digitally and stored in a safe physical folder.

Section 2: Financial Stability

- ☐ **Safe Haven:** I have active checking and savings accounts.
- ☐ **Survival Budget:** I know exactly how much my Four Walls (rent, food, communications (phone/internet), transportation) cost each month.
- ☐ **Savings Seed:** I have at least **$100 to $500** tucked away in my savings account for emergencies.

Section 3: Housing & Logistics

- ☐ **Landing Zone:** I have secured a safe place to sleep, even if it is temporary.
- ☐ **Transit Map:** I can navigate to my workplace and the grocery store using public transportation without getting lost.
- ☐ **Communication Link:** I have a local phone number and a data plan I can afford.

Section 4: Employment & Etiquette

- ☐ **Foothold:** I have secured my first local job (or have completed 50+ applications).
- ☐ **Professional Shift:** I understand the punctuality rule and direct communication style of work in my new home.
- ☐ **Reference:** I have at least one person (supervisor or coworker) who can speak to my work ethic.

Section 5: Healthcare & Well-Being

- ☐ **Coverage Check:** I know if I am covered by provincial health insurance (Canada) or eligible for state-funded or employer-sponsored insurance (US).
- ☐ **Emergency Route:** I know the location of the nearest *urgent care clinic* (for non-life-threatening issues) and the nearest *emergency room* (for life-threatening crises).
- ☐ **Pharmacy Foundation:** I have identified a nearby pharmacy and know how to transfer any essential prescriptions from my home country.
- ☐ **Primary Contact:** I have a list of local community health centers that offer sliding-scale fees based on income for newcomers.

🛠 Tool: Stability to Growth—Your 90-Day Audit

Use this chart to visualize your progress. Most newcomers start in the **Red Zone** and move toward the **Green Zone** by the end of this book.

Level	Status	Healthcare Milestone	Your Current Action
Survival (Red)	Low cash, no job, temporary housing	**Emergency Only:** Identified the nearest hospital and pharmacy.	**Focus:** Day 1–30 Action Plan
Stability (Yellow)	First job secured, bank account open, savings started	**Navigating:** Found a local community health center or urgent care center with sliding-scale fees.	**Focus:** Day 31–60 Action Plan
Foundation (Green)	Steady income, local ID, moving to a long-term lease	**Covered:** Applied for provincial health card (Canada) or learned about employer/state insurance (US).	**Graduation:** You are ready for book 2.

Reflection: From Newcomer to Resident

Take a moment to look back at the day you landed.

- **How much more do you know now than you did then?**
- **How many "scary" things have you already handled** (opening a bank account, taking the bus, the first interview)?

The Immigrant's Secret: The hardest part of the journey is the first 90 days. You have survived the Zero Phase. You are no longer just a visitor; you are a builder. Your future is not something that happens to you, it is something you are now creating with your own hands.

Your Next Step

You have mastered **Survival**. Now it is time to master **Success**.

In ***Book 2: Building Your Financial Fortress***, we will move beyond "just getting by." We will dive deep into:

1. **Cracking the Credit Code:** How to get from zero to a high credit score.
2. **Career Climbing:** How to leave the "survival job" and enter your professional field.
3. **Wealth Building:** Buying your first car, your first home, and investing for your family's future.

CONCLUSION

The First Victory Is Yours

Dear friend,

You have reached the end of book 1, and before you turn the page to the next phase of your journey, I want to pause and speak to you personally.

These first 90 days are not easy. They test your courage, your patience, your identity, and sometimes even your faith. You walked into a new world where nothing felt familiar—new roads, new rules, new systems, and new expectations. Yet, you kept going. You kept reading. You kept learning.

That alone tells me one thing: *you are serious about your future.*

This book was designed to provide the solid ground you need to stand on: your documents, your first bank account, a safe place to sleep, and your first paycheck. By mastering these, you have done the hardest part. You have survived the "Great Transition." Most people will never understand the bravery it takes to start over from zero in a foreign land. But I do. Every immigrant does. That courage is already your first great victory.

The Road Ahead: From Survival to Freedom

While book 1 was about **Survival**, the journey is just beginning. We are not here to help you simply "get by"; we are here to help you *thrive*. Your journey follows a powerful ascent:

- ***Book 2: Building Your Financial Fortress (6–18 Months)*** In the next phase, we move beyond the basics. We will tackle the "invisible" systems of North America. You will learn how to **crack the credit code**, move from a "survival job" into a **career**, and navigate the healthcare and tax systems so they work for you, not against you.
- ***Book 3: Owning Your Future (Year 2+)*** This is where your roots grow deep. We will discuss **wealth building**, purchasing your first home, investing for your children's future, and reaching the ultimate goal: the **Freedom State**. This is the point where you are no longer "fitting in," but leading and contributing as a pillar of your new community.

A Final Word of Encouragement

Do not be discouraged if you still feel like a newcomer. Every giant oak tree was once an acorn that had to struggle through the dark soil before it reached the sun. You are currently in the soil, but you are growing.

> **The Immigrant's Promise:** The sacrifice of your today is the seed of your family's tomorrow. You are not just changing your own life; you are changing the history of your entire bloodline.

Hold your head high. You have the documents in your folder, the money in your bank, and the fire in your heart. You are ready.

Your Support Network

One of the most important lessons in book 1 is that **you do not have to do this alone.** North America is home to thousands of organizations dedicated to helping newcomers succeed. These resources are the hidden infrastructure of your new life.

Below is a list of trusted organizations and programs across the US and Canada. Keep this list in your **Power Folder**.

Essential Government Gateways

These are your primary starting points for legal status and official resources.

- **USCIS (US)** https://www.uscis.gov/ — the official site for all immigration forms, green card information, and citizenship tools.
  Tip: Use their tool to check case processing times.
- **IRCC (Canada)** https://www.canada.ca/en/immigration-refugees-citizenship.html — everything regarding study permits, work permits, and permanent residency.
  Tip: Use the "Find free newcomer services near you" tool to locate help in your city.

Free and Low-Cost Legal Aid

Never navigate complex legal issues alone. These nonprofits offer expert guidance.

- **Immigration Advocates Network (US)**
  https://www.immigrationadvocates.org/ — features a national directory of nonprofit legal service providers.
- **National Immigrant Justice Center (US)**
  https://immigrantjustice.org/ — provides legal consultations for low-income immigrants and refugees.
- **Canadian Council for Refugees (Canada)**
  https://ccrweb.ca —massive network of organizations that advocate for and protect the rights of newcomers in Canada.

Landlord & Tenant Law

Understanding your rights as a renter protects your safety, your money, and your stability. These resources help you learn local laws, resolve disputes, and avoid common housing traps.

United States:

- **State-by-State Landlord–Tenant Laws (Avail)**
  https://www.avail.com/education/laws — A simple directory where you can choose your state and read the exact rules on deposits, repairs, evictions, and lease terms.
- **FindLaw Landlord–Tenant Law Guide**

https://lawyers-.findlaw.com/ — A legally reviewed overview of tenant rights, eviction rules, habitability standards, and discrimination protections, plus links to every state's laws.

- **Legal Information Institute (Cornell Law School)**
  https://www.law.cornell.edu — Clear explanations of landlord obligations, tenant protections, and federal housing laws like the Fair Housing Act.

Canada:

- **Government of Canada – Landlord & Tenant Relations** https://ised-isde.canada.ca/site/ised/ — Explains leases, privacy rights, dispute processes, and links to each province's rental authority.
- **Tenant Rights Canada** https://tenantrights.ca/ — A province-by-province guide to tenant rights, eviction rules, and legal resources across the country.
- **Provincial Housing Authorities** — Each province has its own laws. For example, Ontario's Residential Tenancies Act page (https://www.ontario.ca/page/renting-ontario-your-rights) explains rent increases, eviction rules, and where to get help for that province.

Employment and Career Success

These groups help you move from a survival job to a career.

- **Upwardly Global (US)** https://www.upwardlyglobal.org/ — specializes in helping work-authorized immigrants rebuild their professional careers in the US.
- **COSTI Immigrant Services (Canada)** http://www.costi.org — leading agency in the Greater Toronto Area providing employment training and settlement support.
- **Welcome.US (US)** https://welcome.us/ — national initiative connecting newcomers with local community partners for job connections and school enrollment.

Language and Integration

Learning the local language is your fastest path to freedom.

- **Language Instruction for Newcomers to Canada (LINC) Program (Canada)**
  https://www.canada.ca/en/immigration-refugees-citizenship/services/settle-canada/language-

skills/classes.html — free English and French classes funded by the Canadian government for permanent residents.

- **Catholic Charities (US)** https://www.catholiccharitiesusa.org/ — one of the largest networks providing citizenship education and English as a Second Language (ESL) classes across the US.

Humanitarian and General Support

For when you need immediate help with food, housing, or clothing.

- **International Rescue Committee (IRC) (US)** https://www.rescue.org/ — Operates in over 25 US cities, helping with resettlement, healthcare, and emergency aid.
- **Global Refuge (US)** https://www.globalrefuge.org — Formerly known as Lutheran Immigration and Refugee Service (LIRS), provides social services and advocacy for refugees and migrants of all backgrounds.
- **211 Information Service (US and Canada):** Simply **dial 2-1-1** on your phone. It is a free, confidential service that connects you to local resources for food, housing, and healthcare.

Health and Defense

For protecting your Fortress Fund from medical debt.

Government and Marketplace Health Coverage for Newcomers

- **Medicaid (US) — Free or low-cost health insurance for low-income individuals.** Many immigrants qualify depending on status and state rules. Apply through your state Medicaid office or HealthCare.gov (https://www.healthcare.gov/medicaid-chip/).
- **HealthCare.gov (The Marketplace) (US)** https://www.healthcare.gov — essential for finding plans that

fit your budget to ensure your savings strategy for **Health Care** is aligned.

- **HRSA Data Warehouse (US)**
  https://findahealthcenter.hrsa.gov — Use the *Find a Health Center* tool (HRSA) to locate nearby Federally Qualified Health Centers that offer sliding-scale fees if you are between survival jobs.
- **Provincial Health Insurance (Canada)** — Newcomers must apply for a provincial health card (OHIP, MSP, AHCIP, etc.). Some provinces have a 90-day waiting period. Apply immediately after arrival.
  - Canada Health cards (Canada.ca): https://www.canada.ca/en/health-canada/services/health-cards.html
  - Provincial breakdown: https://canadahealthjournal.ca.

How to Use This Directory

Don't wait for a crisis: Visit these websites now to see what they offer.

Ask for "Newcomer Services": When you call, clearly state, "I am a newcomer and I am looking for [Legal/Job/Language] assistance."

Check Eligibility: Many of these services are free, but some may depend on your immigration status or income level.

You have the map. You have the tools. You have the network.

I am proud of the progress you've made in book 1. I'll see you in ***Book 2: The Financial Fortress***, where we start the 6-to-18-month climb toward your permanent future.

About the Author

Alain Pougom is an IT professional, entrepreneur, and educator dedicated to helping immigrants build stable and successful lives in the United States. Originally from Cameroon, he arrived in America with limited English, a young family, and no clear roadmap—learning the system step by step while navigating housing, work, transportation, and finances in real time.

Through discipline, research, and lived experience, Alain built strong financial habits, achieved excellent credit, gave a safe place to life to his family, and established a career in Information Technology with more than twelve years of experience in infrastructure, systems administration, networking, and enterprise operations.

Driven by a passion for empowering newcomers, Alain created *Motivation + Finance for Freedom in USA*, a platform focused on financial literacy, personal growth, and practical guidance for immigrants and first-generation families. His work centers on helping others avoid common mistakes, make informed decisions early, and build long-term stability with confidence and purpose.

Through his *"Newcomer's Guide to Building a Life in North America"* series, Alain shares the practical, experience-based insights he wishes he had when began his own journey—offering newcomers a clearer path from confusion to confidence, and from survival to opportunity.

Series Page

A Newcomer's Guide to Building a Life in North America

The Complete System

Starting over in a new country is not a single event—it is a process.

This series is designed as a structured path to guide you from uncertainty to stability, and ultimately to long-term financial independence in North America. Each book represents a distinct phase of that journey, building on the one before it.

Book 1 — Surviving the First 90 Days

The Essential Survival Guide for Newcomers in the US and Canada

This is where your journey begins.

In your first 90 days, the objective is clear: establish stability. You focus on the essentials—housing, transportation, banking, income, and understanding how daily life works.

This phase is not about perfection.
It is about adaptation, discipline, and gaining your footing in a new system.

Book 2 — Building Your Financial Fortress

How Newcomers Build Credit, Income, and Financial Stability in North America (6–18 Months)

Once stability is established, the next step is control.

In this phase, you move from reacting to life to structuring it. You will learn how to:

- Build and protect your credit profile
- Stabilize and increase your income
- Eliminate financial leaks and unproductive habits
- Organize your financial systems and documentation
- Position yourself for long-term growth

This is where many newcomers remain stuck—working hard without real progress.
This phase ensures you build a foundation that supports your future.

Book 3 — Owning Your Future

The Practical Guide to Building Wealth, Investing, and Achieving Financial Freedom in North America (Year 2+)

With a solid foundation in place, you are ready to grow.

This phase focuses on ownership, expansion, and long-term strategy. You will learn how to:

- Transition from saving to investing
- Build wealth with intention and discipline
- Navigate homeownership and asset acquisition
- Explore business and income expansion opportunities
- Design a life based on freedom—not survival

This is where your journey transforms.
You are no longer trying to "make it."
You are building a life that works for you.

A Final Word

Each phase matters.

Skipping steps creates stress.

Following the process creates momentum.

Take this journey one stage at a time:

- Survive first
- Then build
- Then own your future

You are not just starting over.
You are building something stronger, wiser, and more intentional than before.

Let's begin.

Continue Your Journey

Finishing this book is not the end of your journey—it is the beginning of your foundation.

Starting over in a new country takes more than courage. It takes information, structure, discipline, and the willingness to keep learning.

If this book has helped you think more clearly, avoid costly mistakes, or feel more prepared for your next steps, stay connected for practical guidance designed specifically for immigrants and first-generation families building a future in North America.

Stay Connected

Follow for educational content on:

- Credit building and money habits
- Financial stability and budgeting
- Career growth and income strategies
- Motivation and long-term planning for newcomers

Motivation + Finance for Freedom in USA

Facebook: *Motivation + Finance for Freedom in USA*
YouTube: *@MotivationFinanceforFreedomUSA*
TikTok: *@MotivationFinanceforFreedomUSA*
Instagram: *@MotivationFinanceforFreedomUSA*

Join the Community

Get updates, future resources, and upcoming book releases.

Visit: books.propelitsolutions.com

Email: books@propelitsolutions.com

www.ingramcontent.com/pod-product-compliance
Lightning Source LLC
LaVergne TN
LVHW051932051126
851857LV00020B/2071